# THE WINE GAME

## THE ARISTOCRACY OF THE CORK AND VILLAINY

A personal view of a serious subject
but not without levity

by
Arthur Woods

Published in Great Britain in 2010 by Arthur Woods

Copyright © Arthur Woods, 2010

Designed and typeset by Helen Joubert Design

Printed and bound in Great Britain by
CPI Antony Rowe, Chippenham and Eastbourne

The moral right of the authors has been asserted.

All rights reserved.
Without limiting the rights under copyright reserved above,
no part of this publication may be reproduced, stored or introduced into a
retrieval system, or transmitted, in any form or by any means (electronic,
mechanical, photocopying, recording or otherwise), without the prior written
permission of both the copyright owner and the publisher of this book.

A CIP catalogue record for this book is available from
the British Library.

ISBN 978 0 9546773 3 6

Cover image: *The Wine Game* by Heather Stirling

Also by Arthur Woods:
*A Huckster: Fifty years on the roads of Europe and elsewhere*
*Paul of Tarsus: an enigma enshrouded in a mystery*
*From the Shankill to the Shenandoah – the scotch Irish in America*
*The Anglo Irish – Giants in the Land of Lilliput*

Copper Beech Vineyard
Black Hill
Lindfield
West Sussex RH16 2HF

Tel: 01444 483084
Fax: 01444 450654
E-mail: woodsarthur@yahoo.co.uk
www.reallyreadablewriter.co.uk

# SIGNIFICANT QUOTATIONS

*"Half the wines made in the Midi are sold to shippers in Bordeaux and Burgundy to emerge in bottles with valuable labels."*
*"The better Clarets often contain a bit of Algerian"*
*"Experts cannot tell Claret from Plonk."*
    (Quotations from witnesses at the Great Bordeaux Fraud Trial 1974)

*"All right I'll buy the place as long as I don't have to drink the bloody stuff!"*
    (Lord Cowdray on being asked to buy Château Latour in 1962)

*"It is plain that few of those who imagine they are drinking the first growths of Bordeaux can even be drinking the second. The most extensive operations of this nature (blending) are carried out at Bordeaux with the wines we now call Claret, but not one thousandth part of which are of good quality or unmixed in someway, and the one half of which perhaps are not French but Spanish wine."*
    (Encyclopaedia Britannica 1842)

*"Of the Château Lafite 1795 (a fine year) that made up with Hermitage was the best liked of any of that year."*
    (Nathaniel Johnston. Bordeaux Wine Shipper 1807)

*"There is a particular manufacture called 'travail del'Anglaise' which consists of adding to each hogshead of Bordeaux wine 3 to 4 gallons of Alicant or Benecarlo, half a gallon of stum wine, and sometimes a small quantity of Hermitage."*

(J Henderson in his 'History of Ancient and Modern Wines' 1824)

*"The great problem for wine writers is that they can't bite the hand that feeds them. They are dependent on Château owners opening bottles to taste for free, or inviting them to dinners of old vintages."*

(Anthony Hanson MW)

# CONTENTS

| | |
|---|---|
| 1. ADVENT | 1 |
| 2. THE BEGINNING | 9 |
| 3. THE DEVELOPMENT | 13 |
| 4. THE BURGUNDIAN SLOPES OF THE CÔTE D'OR | 22 |
| 5. SHERRY AND THE PROVINCE OF JEREZ | 31 |
| 6. THE EXPATRIATES AND OTHERS | 43 |
| 7. THE SUPREMACY OF THE MEDOC | 65 |
| 8. THE 1855 CLASSIFICATION OF THE MEDOC | 77 |
| 9. LES QUAI DES CHARTRONS | 83 |
| 10. THE SHOT CALLERS OF THE CHARTRONNAIS | 97 |
| 11. THE MEDIEVAL ROADS OF FRANCE | 108 |
| 12. PORTUGAL, A FEW REMINDERS | 111 |
| 13. PORTWINE? ANYBODY CAN MAKE IT | 116 |
| 14. THE CRITICAL PATH OF THE PORTWINE MAN | 123 |
| 15. THE FACTORY HOUSE | 126 |
| 16. MADEIRA | 130 |
| 17. MADEIRA: THE MAKING OF THE WINE | 134 |
| 18. MADEIRA AFTER THE RETURN OF CHARLES II IN 1662 | 136 |
| 19. THE EXPATRIATES OF MADEIRA | 139 |
| 20. MADEIRA FROM 1920 TO THE 21ST CENTURY | 144 |
| 21. MARSALA | 149 |

| | |
|---|---|
| 22. WINE FRAUDS DE NOS JOURS | 154 |
| 23. THE WINE THAT DARED NOT SPEAK ITS NAME | 158 |
| 24. HOW ARE THE MIGHTY FALLEN? | 161 |
| 25. BEAUJOLAIS NOUVEAU – THE PERPETUAL VIRGIN | 164 |
| 26. AUSTRIA AND ITS COSY RELATIONSHIP WITH DIETHYLENE GLYCOL | 171 |
| 27. THE GREAT BORDEAUX FRAUD | 177 |
| 28. THE RODENSTOCK JEFFERSON AFFAIR | 183 |
| 29. POSTSCRIPT | 190 |
| SELECTED FURTHER READING | 195 |

# 1

## ADVENT

"Stay me with flagons, comfort me with apples for I am sick of love." Thus spoke whoever wrote "The Song of Solomon". The wisdom of 750 BC, and today for that matter, I write this, in admiration, tempered with awe of that tight-knit group which *"laboured in the vineyard"* and were an unbroken line back to Solomon and much earlier. Some soiled their hands, some did not, and they worked *en famille*, which gave strength and occasional weakness. It is also a very personal view. I was never in the wine trade, though very much on the periphery which sharpens objectivity and develops clear-sightedness. A tiny vineyard planted in 1978, partly to learn about viticulture the dirty-handed way, and so that I felt less of a charlatan, as I was writing from time short pieces about wine in France, Italy and other countries. One conclusion I reached, and I am sure not the first, was the only way to guarantee a profit in the wine game was to make corks, labels and bottles. All others, the commission men, the merchants, the shippers, the marketing people did well to very well. It may be a little coarse but by no means unfair to draw a parallel with those who made the best living out of the Klondike, Californian and other Gold Rushes. Not the diggers, but the suppliers of food, booze and whores. There is a dry humour among some in or associated with the wine trade to be considered as a sort of *aristocracy of the cork*. It also adds to one's experience to have been drinking wines that varied from the products of Bordeaux great vineyards to the stomach-wrenching wines of the Balkans.

Many Grande Châteaux owners became exemplars of that aphorism "How to make a small fortune? First start with a large one." But money was rarely considered when ownership of a Bordeaux Grand Cru, or any wine estate in the 1855 Medoc Classification was on offer. For as the owner of a great vineyard your name might be known throughout much of the world. Whereas, should the source of your wealth come from the manufacture of tee-shirts and baseball caps in Lille, who would have heard of you north of the Pas de Calais or south of Amiens? Similarly a master butcher in Yorkshire might be able to sign a cheque for a million pounds but still have no social cachet outside of Leeds. But to be the major shareholder in a Premier League football club just around the corner, he is automatically promoted to the rank of bigwig or a somebody. Such is fame; sometimes as fragile as a soap-bubble; sometimes as strong as Sheffield steel.

So how did this book come to be written? The germination was long and sometimes uncertain. There were dramatic events that preserved the seed over two generations or more, yet provided green shoots that turned into a sturdy plant screaming to be noticed. My lifelong interest in wine and just about everything connected with it stems from 3 stories; 2 of them about wartime Italy, the 3rd about Czechoslovakia during the period of what was known as the Cold War; and wine is central to all 3.

In November 1943 the 8th Army was halted by atrocious weather on the south banks of the River Sangro on the north east coast of Italy near Ortona. What had been a gentle stream one week earlier was now a raging torrent 75 yards wide. The tanks could not cross until a Bailey bridge was slung across by the Royal Engineers, neither could the infantrymen or the gunners. But there was solace in the fortified farmhouse which sheltered many of the foot soldiers; for in the cellars were two huge wine barrels, immensely old, each perhaps 20 feet long and 8 feet high; and they held red wine. So half a company of soldiers with a tendency towards violence, and getting more bored by the hour found themselves temporarily in charge of unlimited quantities of wine and decided to live for the day, *carpe diem*. Clearly the farm was a co-operative to which the peasants had brought their small harvests for vinification the previous August, and it had not yet been racked after fermentation. Little did the peasants know what God had abandoned them to when the Germans reached the area. So the soldiers passed the time pleasantly enough, keeping their pint tea mugs full from a wooden tap from which flowed red wine that might not even have won prizes in Moscow. No matter, for once, Dionysus had smiled on them. Then with no warning the flow became a trickle and a trickle nothing. Whereupon a soldier enraged at being denied his lawful ration became very vexed and attacked the barrel with bayonet and rifle butt and breached it. A small breach under pressure of wine became a large one until half the front of the barrel came away followed by a torrent of wine and what seemed to be a large bungle of rags. But it was not rags it was a body; a woman's body; headless. Even the hardened soldiers were shocked. Discreet enquiries followed from a few peasants who had remained in the village. "So that's where she was all the time. Her bloke done her in and dropped her through a hole he'd cut in the top. That barrel had not been cleaned for years nor was it likely to be." Happily the other barrel remained intact and full. Peace was restored and so was the vino rosso. It was another week before the river could be crossed.

 The second story relates to events 9 months later. In

August 1944 after a hard slog north, following the end of the six months battle for Monte Cassino, my regiment was camped alongside the River Elsa, deep in that part of Tuscany later to be called by travel-writers "Chiantishire." It was much favoured from the 1960's onwards by the British middle-classes. To identify the area more closely, the towers of San Gimignano were about 10 miles to the north east and Siena 10 miles to the south east. The Germans were slowly retreating north from Florence, but not before blowing-up all the bridges over the River Arno, save the medieval Ponte Vecchio. We were likely to be resting for a few days, so another young officer and myself were ordered to scour the countryside and persuade the peasantry to sell us food and drink, to add to our meagre army rations. Naturally they had hidden most things but had left out a few hens and ducks for bargaining purposes. First the Germans, and then us; but at least we neither killed the men nor raped the women. We found an empty, quite elegant manor house with Palladian pretensions in the midst of lush vineyards, and which yielded an astounding find. But there was a snag. As the Germans retreated they left behind presents for the unwary, looting soldiers such as us. These were cunningly concealed booby-traps, which could at least blow-off a foot or something even more highly valued! So, scared out of our wits, and uselessly clutching the genital areas, we moved slowly into the house; and found the cellar – and what a cellar! It was full of bottles of Chianti; the old-style, straw-clad, broad-based called "Fiaschi". Such as were to be found in many British living-rooms turned into table lamps. We loaded as many as would fill our jeep, and had another look. There were seven wooden boxes, one with the top broken, and in it bottles of wine bearing what seemed like French labels, which meant nothing to us, but back at the camp they did to another officer of more mature years, who had recently returned, having recovered from a severe wound suffered a few months earlier. He picked-up a bottle, looked at the label and to use an expression widely used now, but not then, he was gob smacked. "You have liberated seven dozen bottles of Château Lafite 1929, probably the greatest claret of which many people already considered the greatest Bordeaux vintage of the century. You are a thief" he continued, "but you deserve a medal of some sort". How did he know this but not me? Because he was a taster and buyer for an illustrious London Merchants that only imported from the Medoc. We opened and drank two bottles the next day, and for me the taste of such a wine was a seminal experience; the first steps on a wine Odyssey, which continues today, 65 years later. In fact after the Lafite was finished; it did not last very far north of Florence, and as far as wine was concerned, I drank nothing but vin ordinaire and worse, Australian Burgundy. Though the nadir of my drinking during that six years after the war was Algerian red; 15% alcohol at three pounds six shillings £3.6s a case, delivered free within inner London. Now that really *did* do your head in!

Sixteen years were to pass before the scene for the 3rd story was set in Czechoslovakia, a country in which I was frequently to travel between September 1956 and August 1968 when the Russians invaded that unfortunate country. On August 21st I had reached my hotel in central Prague only a few hours earlier. During the night I heard shouting and screaming and a maid told me that the Russians had landed on the Airport. I packed-up, paid and motored due east to Ostrava, my ultimate destination which was the Tatra Motor Company. As I drove-up a Polish motorised battalion passed me and before I could gain entrance to the plant an armoured division had passed on its way to Prague.

Hundreds of workers stood silently outside; nobody waving, nobody cheering; stunned. I parked and a man who I recognised as the General Manager strolled over. "You won't be surprised I had forgotten you were coming," he said. "It's all over, the Russians will make us pay for this invasion and there will be no investment for years. Contact us in a year's time to find out the position." Two years work gone down the plughole I thought.

Anyway, I decided to drive the 100 miles to Brno to see my friends; perhaps for the last time and then retreat to Austria and home. Though I *did* go to Prague first, to see what was happening there, but that is another story. It was another 21 years before Czechoslovakia was delivered from the tyranny of Russia. Caused by the fall of the Berlin Wall. I had been visiting Czechoslovakia about 6 times a year since 1956; and as you do in what had been a civilised nation for centuries, friends are made and acquaintances met. They were an unusual bunch, well educated, youngish and not as you would expect. Not doctors, journalists, academics, scientists or high-flyers. That is what they should have been; but a vicious Communist Government full of malice and hatred of the middle classes, the bourgeoisie had robbed them of their jobs. A bigger crime was to have left the country in 1939 to fight in the British Armed Forces; because you were bound to have brought back with you decadent ideas of freedom and liberty, both inimical to the Communist dialectic so their punishment was poor housing, low paid labouring jobs, poor schooling for their children, who were also denied entrance to the universities. We met frequently for talks and drinks, mostly excellent Czech pilsner beer but also the wines grown in and around the village of Hustopece some 15 miles south of Brno towards the Austrian border at Mikoluv. The 68 year-old mother of one friend had to get up at 4am to catch the bus to Brno where from 6am to 3pm she did a cleaning job. She rarely got home before 5pm.

It was in Hustopece in March 1956 that my friends and I met in a small wine cellar owned by one of them, and we were having a good go at the 1955 vintage. The traditional grapes of southern Moravia are Sylvaner and Traminer which when blended made a refreshing and pleasant drink, ideal for quaffing in quantity. This was a place where talkers could feel safe from informers and government spies; which was just as well. The young local policeman was also there but he was regarded as "one of us". The talk that night was particularly loose as one of them had just lost his job; which in a country where <u>nobody</u> lost his job; where 3 people normally did one person's job made him an "unperson"; for there was no unemployment money. Suddenly a pair broke into the Horst Wessel, the Hitler Youth song. The policeman started to wail, then shout, and discharged the whole magazine of his hand-gun into the cellar roof. Who could have known that in 1942, in front of him, his sister and his mother, his father and two others had been hanged. Everybody was silent. To be heard singing the Horst Wessel was a serious crime to be rewarded by a long prison sentence but the cop's sobbing ceased as people consoled him, for he valued his membership of this group of subversives, and he kept quiet about the happening of that night. I met him many times between then and August 1968, and continued as a messenger boy between my friends and their friends in the UK, bearing tapes, letters and small gifts.

From 1950 onwards, I started on my journeyings through Europe west and east; from Portugal to Moscow; from France to Sicily; taking in the Levant and much of the Middle East as well, carrying out my work as an international engineer and sales director. Never far from the vineyards of nearly every wine growing country. My work also became an Odyssey in search of Dionysus. How could a man be so lucky? The roads of Europe took me everywhere, for I travelled mostly by road, and a car then was the most flexible means of transport. Bordeaux knew me many times. So did the Loire along all its length. The Sâone, the Rhône and the Rhine, knew me better than the Thames, the Avon and the Severn. Alsace with perhaps the world's most underrated wines I encountered frequently also the German vineyards of the Rheingau, Rheinhessen and the Pfalz Palatinate. Time out of number I admired the 22 miles and scarcely 22000 acres of the Burgundian Côte d'Or. This would have satisfied most people but over the Alps were the lovely unregarded vineyards of the Swiss Valais and then over the Italian Alps were the northern misty vineyards of Piedmont with its massive, meaty Barolos. It was an Odyssey that could never be completed for there was still Spain with its reliable Riojas improved out of recognition by the Domecq family when in the 1960's they bought into the Rioja business and introduced much needed discipline into the wine making. What a life and what sultanic opulence I enjoyed as I dined and wined at the tables of Europe for over 50 years.

# 2

# THE BEGINNING

The wine itself is not the central narrative, it is the people, the growers, the sellers, the entrepreneurs, the go-betweens who have always imposed their personalities and influence on this staple of civilisation. As to origins, there are more stories told about that than you could shake a stick at. I prefer to accept the one about the clay vessel in which grapes for eating had been stored and then forgotten. In the fullness of time these fermented into a liquid. Greatly daring somebody put his finger in to taste it, liked it, drank some, then drank a lot until he was hammered and had a hangover. From then on it was downhill all the way. This has none of the banality of Adam receiving the apple from Eve and much more likely. Tradition names the fruit eaten by both as an apple but a grape would have been much more interesting. That more than any other fruit has forever hastened mankind towards perdition. Who can imagine a great industry based on a Cox's Orange Pippin? And the place where this earth-shaking event took place? As good as any, I suppose, is somewhere between the Tigris and the Euphrates. For was not this river, the fourth along with Pison, Gihon and Hiddekel to flow out of Eden? And the time of 8000 BC seems to satisfy most of the pundits. From that unpromising start, people hardly out of the hunter/gatherer stage started the cultivation of the wild grape, vitis-vinifera sativa (vitisvinifera for short).

We should be indebted to that first vinous piss artist, for without him there would have been no God Dionysus (or

Bacchus if you were Roman). There are only about 35 species of vine (though thousands of cultivars), and the European one is vitis vinifera, which laboriously over many centuries reached the European Continent. Firstly, probably by the Phoenicians, great sailors and traders, who left what is now the Lebanon to make landfall somewhere near Cadiz in Spain and not too far from Jerez de la Frontera, the home of sherry. Secondly, the Greeks who colonised Sicily and Marseilles in about 500/600 BC. Thirdly, and in a disciplined and businesslike way, the Romans. Caesar's conquest of Gaul brought the vine speedily to France; for wine was as necessary to his legionnaires as bread. It came the easy way, by water; following the Rhône, the Loire, the Sâone, the Dordogne and the Moselle. Fruit growing as opposed to fruit gathering would at best have been sporadic and it took many generations before wines were made of stable and sumptuous quality that only the rich could afford; and about which a coarse-mouthed fellow could boast to his coarse-mouthed friends that his palate was so sensitive it could detect in the wine they were drinking the nature of the grape-picker, be she virgin, matron or whore.

The Egyptians, early sophisticates in market development, wasted no time in exporting their surpluses. They were way ahead of their Mediterranean neighbours in mercantile affairs. Their history offers plenty of information on vineyard establishment in temple precincts; and it would be surprising if they were not exporting wine both to Greece and Etruscan Italy, before that civilised people disappeared. Wheat also, probably accompanied the wine. When the soldiers of Islam reached Egypt in the 7th century AD, sword in one hand, copy of the Koran in the other, they would have found many vineyards in the Nile Delta to destroy and keep faith with the anti-alcohol Islamic strictures.

With the passage of time, many wars, many plagues, urbanisation in the form of the settlements, villages and towns, a whole structure of life based on law was created round the growing of the grape. Villages sold their surpluses to the towns, the towns built shops for the retail trade, and merchants travelled widely with their wine samples. By the 18th century that happy band of brothers, the growers, the wholesalers, bottlers, négociants and even the scribblers were united in a close-knit society of interdependency. The scientists were not far behind, and even treated with respect after the ruinous disasters of phylloxera in the late 19th century.

By the turn of the 20th century a huge chemical industry arose to deal with the grapes many predators, botrytis oidium and others. The sugar industry also benefited, for the wine growers, especially the Burgundians, have always had an uneasy and sometimes shameful relationship with sugar. The labourers in the vineyard, at least in Bordeaux and notably in the Medoc turned themselves into gentry "The aristocracy of the cork." We must pray it will not turn into an "aristocracy of the screw-top." It used to be said by the cynical Irish in Dublin, masters of the putdown, "You may brew but you may not bake." Perhaps in Bordeaux, along the Quai des Chartrons among the merchants in their grand if shabby houses you may occasionally hear someone murmur "on peut faire du vin mais pas du pain".

And now what? For there is a relentless drive to expand in the wine industry especially globally. Already the suspicious French, conservative as only the descendants of those who toiled the soil for centuries can be, have found merit in the wines of California and Australia and invested heavily there. A huge market for wine is very much on the cards in Asia, especially in India and China. Industry generally has a growing middle class, eager to get drunk on European wines. As I write, I read that Lafite is planning to plant 65 acres in China. And when India and China are growing decent wine, as they are bound to, where will their surpluses go? To Europe, as did the surpluses of Egypt.

# 3

# THE DEVELOPMENT

The future for wine may have been India and China, but much history had to be made before that huge leap to Asia could come to pass. To say that history could be ignored at our peril is perhaps rather dramatic; but to ignore it is certainly stupid; and today too many half-educated teachers barely pay lip service to it in the curriculum of pupils. Without giving it intense study, and it is a gripping subject, how can one understand the closeness with which medieval England became linked with medieval France or at least that part bordered by the Atlantic Ocean and a line from Rouen through Normandy, Brittany, Gascony, virtually to the Spanish border. None of which accepted the authority of the French Kings. France did not become a unified country, defined by its current borders until the English and Burgundians were defeated at the end of the 100 years war in the middle of the 15th century. Henry Plantagenet, better known as Henry II married Eleanor of Aquitaine in 1152 and she brought with her as her dowry most of Western France. So the English Crown owned much of France for 300 years including Bordeaux and what was to become later the most famous wine growing area of the world. This historical fact explains the influence that the Anglo Saxon Protestants (and not a few Anglo Irish) exacted over Bordeaux and the Medoc. Even in some ways today. Who said "History is bunk?"

England, already a maritime power, gained greatly from

possession of Bordeaux and the long Atlantic coast with its many ports. Bordeaux, at the confluence of the Dordogne and Garonne Rivers, which merged into the wide waters of the Gironde estuary, was the natural shipping port for the export of wine and other products. Its merchants exploited its monopoly powers ruthlessly when La Rochelle fell to France in 1230 and Bordeaux became the monopoly supplier of wine to England for over 200 years until 1453 when the French took Bordeaux also. But the English remained popular with the Bordelaise who welcomed their soldiers after the final battle of the Spanish Peninsular War in 1813 when they crossed into France and into Bordeaux. The people considered them liberators from the tyranny of Napoleon.

While the English controlled so much of Western France, the small ports in the many estuaries were alive with boats shipping wine to England. The people of England, Scotland and Ireland had a terrible thirst for French wines, and by mid 14th century from Bordeaux alone the equivalent of more than 100 million bottles a year were shipped and to a population of no more than 4 millions. That was about 12 bottles per head, per year; which was the consumption per head in the UK in 1950. The bloke in the boat circa 1350; the man in the van now.

The boozing habits of the British has a long history; does nothing change? The great paradox that determined Bordeaux as the wine province of the future is, that climatically and agriculturally it was the wrong place. If you wanted large harvests, then the grapes needed plenty of hot days, little rain and cold (but not too cold) winters; and the places for that were Provence or the Midi *not* Medoc in Bordeaux. Moreover wine was grown in the Midi long before it was in Bordeaux. So despite Bordeaux being the wrong place, the joker in the pack, the place that decided *where* the wine, as an industry should be developed was England because it was easier to get there than to transport it to any place within France itself. Such ease of transportation was denied to the growers in Burgundy and the south. Think of large barrels full of wine, slopping about and probably leaking; primitive wooden carts and wheels without bearings, pulled by horses or more likely oxen; and robbery. The luxury of sea travel would have been the motor road of its day. It was later, much later, that the suitability of the Medoc and adjoining areas emerged as the almost perfect place, despite apparent climate deficiencies and a cast-iron guarantee of 3 poor vintages in every 10; but the saving grace was the gentle maritime climate and the Gulf Stream which in England and Ireland gives a mild Winter.

Wine is full of paradoxes. Of all crops it is the one that makes the smallest demands on the soil. Indeed where wine grows well it is likely that other crops, wheat, barley, oats, potatoes or carrots would do badly. Wine grown on poor soil, as in the Medoc and much of Burgundy plenty of pebbles, gravel and little soil, do well. It will produce huge vintages on rich soil of high alcoholic, coarse-flavoured wine without delicacy, finesse or bouquet. In the Medoc the soil nearest the river where the grapes grow in profusion gives only mediocre wines. But the slopes where the soil is thin with subsoil of clay rich in iron oxide make the wines which give the Medoc its reputation for quality beyond others and ridiculously high prices; but nobody forces a buyer to buy; there is no shortage of cheaper wine. It took centuries before this knowledge was commonplace among the vignerons, maybe because they knew no other wine than their own. Even today you will have difficulty in finding a Bordeaux wine in Burgundy or a Loire wine in Alsace. It is not that the growers think wine from another area is bad (even though he does); he just does not wish to raise doubt among the locals. It was well into the 18th century before the reputation for making the best red wines in France was firmly established. The extent of the Bordeaux vineyards has been virtually unchanged for generations. In 1950 it was given as 287000 acres. Yet if we consider the wines of incomparable quality grown on the left bank of the Gironde from St Estéphe in the north, to Pessac in the south, the area of growth is hardly greater than the 22,000 acres of Burgundy between Fixin on the Côte de Nuits and Santenay on the Côte de Beaune. On the other side of the estuary, Le Blayais, sound wines are made, but are forever doomed to be poor relations of Le Medocais over the water. But that is the position today. In the 18th century it was common for the Regency Bucks to drink the young wines, within a year of fermentation. It was years before the growers, or some of them, observed that ageing in oak barrels started changes in the wine's character. In colour, in finesse, in tannin reduction, in acid reduction and in emergence of the powerful bouquet, which of all the qualities of claret is the most memorable, and that was before bottling, which was crude and unhygienic.

Wine was generally shipped in cask to various destination ports and on to the taverns to be sold direct from the cask. But the streetwise London shippers saw much Value Added by bottling in their warehouses; since the growers had neither the skill nor the inclination nor the capital to invest in bottling plants.

Bottles crudely made from poor quality glass were available from the 14th century. Though the Romans and earlier the Phoenicians, had made glass containers for wine. Closure was always the difficulty, and it was not before the 15th century that corks carefully made from the cork oaks of Portugal and Spain caused dramatic changes to the bottled wine, especially to its maturity. Without the cork would there have been champagne? Cork is of course wood, and it repels moisture, while at the same time admitting tiny quantities of air very slowly measured in years. Another paradox, before the oxygen that enters the bottle finally turns the wine into vinegar, it gives ageing, maturity and all the delightful qualities to be expected from a claret of note for which £1200 a case may have been paid. So before reliable corking and accurate bottle making which was usually done in Northern Europe, wine quality was irregular, unreliable and very often undrinkable.

It would be erroneous to confuse the 14th century red wine with the claret of today. Even the name is confusing. While the English held the west of France it was called "clairette", an old French term for a light coloured wine. By the 18th century it received the slight abbreviation to "claret", which came easier to the English speaker. It was not only light coloured, which suggests it was pressed before the juice had taken up much of the skins colour, but it was highly acidic, suggesting the wine was moving towards its natural state of vinegar rather fast. I fancy there were not many wine snobs in 14th century England, but what the English *did* like was red wine that not only looked strong but *was* strong. The customer is always right, isn't he? So the Bordelaise had no objection to doctoring wine as long as it was done by them and sold under their brand so to speak. They would not tolerate the "up country" strong French reds penetrating the cosy arrangement they had with their best customer. In this restriction of trade they were outstandingly successful. One of the wines used to put beef into the Bordeaux was the vin noire de Cahors whose vineyards were about 100 miles east of Bordeaux. A few pints of grape spirit was often added to each casks so that the customer would not complain about lack of strength.

There was a respected writer of the first half of the 20th century named Mr H Warner-Allen who in 1950 published "A Contemplation of Wine." It is a very good read and I bought it in 1951. He was a gentleman writer of the old school, and knew where to put a comma or a semi-colon, and was old enough to have known Professor George Saintsbury of blessed memory (notes on a Cellar book 1920). The book impressed, particularly the piece about Cahors and its strong black wines. Twenty years later while motoring with my wife in south west France we stopped in Roc-amadour at the Hôtel de Lion d'Or in which he, in about 1950 expressly stayed to taste Cahors wine. The hotel patron was a boy when Warner-Allen was there and got very excited and friendly when I waved the book at him. His father was the patron in 1950. He had no Cahors wine but directed us to M Brossier's Château de Bonnecoste some 20 miles away whose wines it was, that was so highly praised in the book. The vineyard is in the Departement of Lot. M Brossier was in his kitchen watching the Wimbledon Ladies Singles Final with his family but tore himself away to welcome me. The piece about Château Bonnecoste is rather long but here is a shortened version, which gives the flavour of an earlier generation of writers. They were more leisured times.

> "*At Roc-amadour I expressed my regret to the obliging manager of the Hôtel de Lion d'Or that there were no local wines of account in his neighbourhood of the Lot. He referred to two entries in his wine list, one of which was Château de Bonnecoste 1937. The manager said if you just call he will see*

*you, his wine is the only fine one grown in Lot, and he is the patron; and Château de Bonnecoste is his creation."*

*"I tried the red and it was a revelation. It had some kinship with a St Emilion of quality, but it was darker, fuller-bodied combined with an aristocratic bouquet; that velvety texture one is wont to associate with a great Burgundy. Its distinctive feature was the attractive grape flavour, fairly perceptible in certain years of Château Margaux, and conspicuous in the red Loire wines of Chinon and Bourgeuil, which seem to lack the breeding of Bonnecoste. It is often described by reference to the scent of a raspberry; munch a raspberry and at the same time smell a violet; and the resultant taste-smell will approximate to it; though in the wine it is more subtle and refined."*

*"Next day I drove some twenty miles to the Domaine of de Bonnecoste, the home of this interesting wine, situated on a lonely plateau in the commune of Calès. M Brossier warned by telephone was awaiting me and after completing the formality of selling a cow, seemed as pleased to show me his wines as a painter to display his pictures to an art lover. His domaine consists of 1500 acres; much of it rocky and picturesque. Only 25 acres are under vines; For M Brossier works in his vineyard making his wines, matures them, bottles them, and markets them almost single handed, apart from family assistance. M Brossier is officially recognised as the only grower in the Departement whose produce ranks with that of renowned vineyards. There are no vines on his land other than those noble plants on which the renown of the greatest Clarets and Sauternes depend. Untiring perseverance in a system of trial and error has brought into being a wine worthy of a connoisseur's attention. He arrayed for my inspection as of a guard of honour five bottles. It was the red Bonnecoste of 1928 that interested me, and it came to me as a*

*startling surprise. There are few of the finer growths of Claret of which I have not tried; at least one specimen of the 1928 vintage. Much was expected of it, but to this day pretty well all of them remain dumb, hard and generally disappointing. Not one of them has come up to expectation. The Bonnecoste 1928 was exactly what we had hoped that the 1928 Clarets would be when they were ripe and in full maturity. This bouquet was delightfully delicate and flowery, its softness saved from any suspicion of mawkishness by a refreshing touch of acid, and the sweetness of its after-taste promised even longer life and a higher degree of excellence.*

*I asked M Brossier how he had performed this miracle of producing on the most unpromising of sites with a tiny isolated vineyard, a wine that might bear comparison with wines of the best report. His main discovery after years of patient research was that his wines naturally partaking to some extent in the rough coarseness of the ordinary Cahor wines, have a great quantity of superfluities and waste products to get rid of in the lees before they could claim to be wines of quality then maturing had to be long and thorough and therefore as slow as possible. M Brossier owed to Pasteur the knowledge that the development of a wine in the wood is conditioned by the amount of oxygen it takes up through the staves of the cask. In a small cask the operation is accelerated, since the surface of the wines against the staves and therefore more or less in contact with the outer air is greater in proportion to the contents of the barrel than it is in a larger receptacle. M Brossier slows down the process by maturing his red wine in muids and demi-muids; casks of larger capacity than the barriques of Bordeaux so that the oxygen takes longer to permeate their contents and he is able to keep the wine improving in the wood year after year, until every trace of impurity has been shed to the satisfaction of his fastidious taste, which he finds a safer guide than any chemical analysis."*

Well, after reading that astounding, overpowering adoration of M Brossier's wine (I had read it again in the Lion d'Or), I felt the least I could do was buy a case of his 1959, the oldest he had in bottle. If Mr Warner-Allen bought any of this extraordinary wine *sans pareille*, he did not say. The wines he offered for tasting were pleasing though high in tannin. Back home, and after a week or two we opened a bottle and found it lacking a bouquet of any sort or finesse but mighty in tannin. Indeed, to use Mr Warner-Allen's own words about the 1928 Clarets "it was dumb, hard and disappointing." During the next few years I kept taking another go at M Brossier's 1959, but sadly, the last was no better than the first. I had proved to have been as dumb as his wine. But I had found him to be charming and that excused everything. I began to wonder, was this all a fantasy? Did M Brossier or Mr Warner-Allen exist and had I read his book? Now, I had in my possession Michael Broadbent's massive and authoritative tome of 1980 "The Great Vintage Wine Book." Here is his verdict on the 1928 vintage in the Medoc. "A monumental year. Of all the vintages of this decade the most massively constructed, and holding best." He listed 26 Châteaux, many of them tasted several times. Now what are you to make of that? Mr Warner-Allen said the 1928 Clarets were rubbish. Mr Broadbent says they are great. M Brossiers 1959 I found poor. Mr Broadbent says 1959 was "masculine and magnificent". I felt like many a Jesuit who had lost his faith and joined the Communist Party. Or the subject of one of Hillaire Belloc's "Cautionary Tales."

# 4

# THE BURGUNDIAN SLOPES OF THE CÔTE D'OR

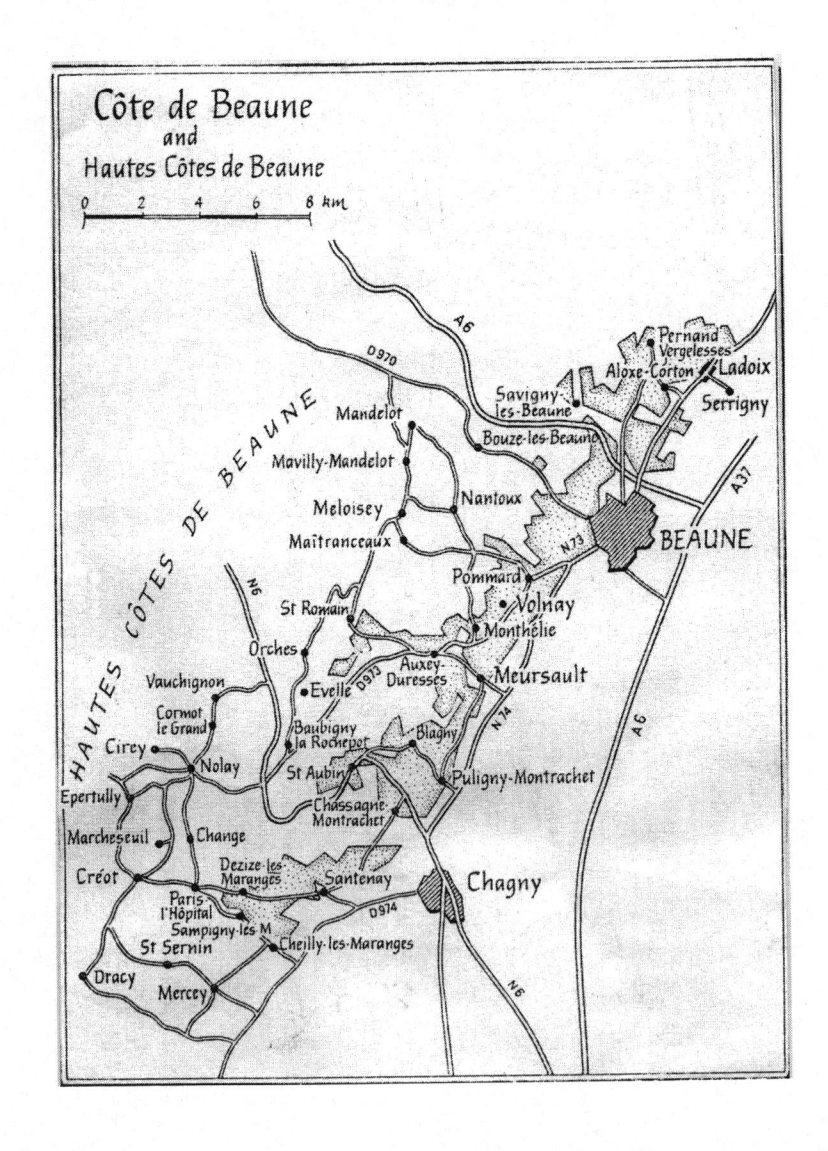

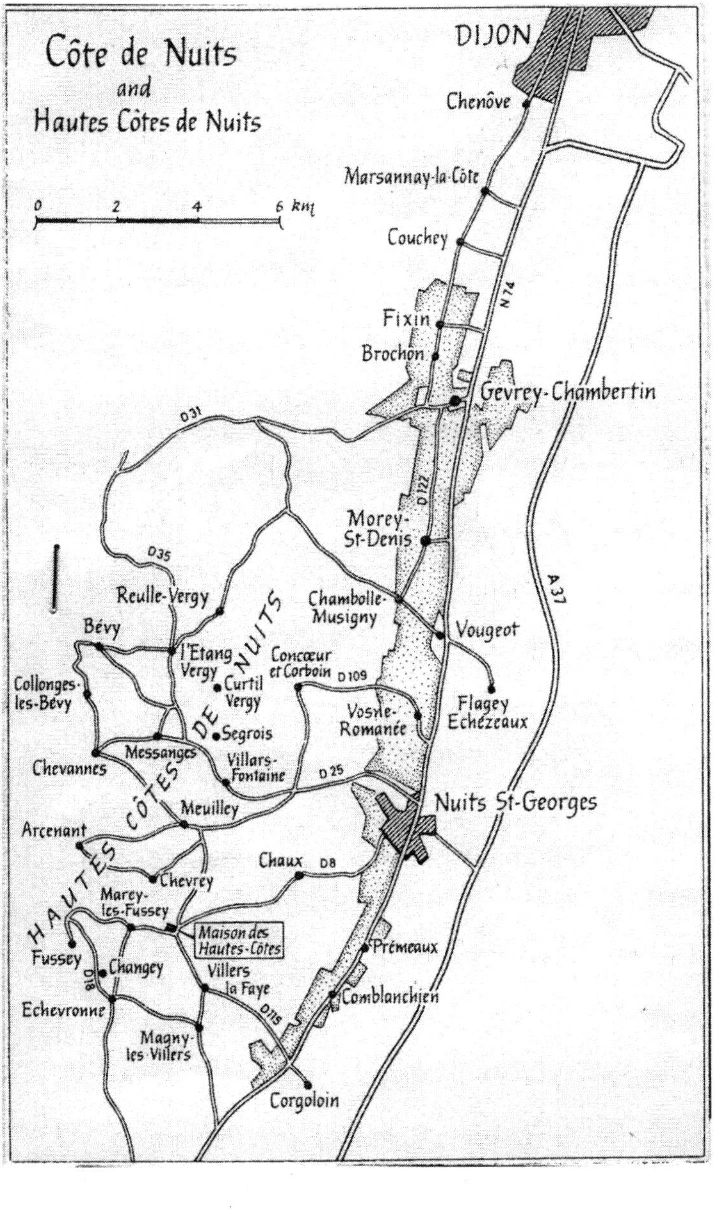

Côte de Nuits
and
Hautes Côtes de Nuits
0 2 4 6 km
DIJON
Chenôve
Marsannay-la-Côte
Couchey
Fixin
Brochon
N74
Gevrey-Chambertin
D31
D122
Morey-St-Denis
D35
Reulle-Vergy
Chambolle-Musigny
Vougeot
A37
Bévy
l'Etang Vergy
Concœur et Corboin
D109
Curtil Vergy
Flagey Echézeaux
Collonges-les-Bévy
Vosne-Romanée
Segrois
Messanges
Villars-Fontaine
D25
Chevannes
Nuits St-Georges
Meuilley
Arcenant
HAUTES CÔTES DE NUITS
Chaux
D8
Chevrey
Marey-les-Fussey
Maison des Hautes-Côtes
Prémeaux
Fussey
D18
Changey
Villers la Faye
Comblanchien
D115
Echevronne
Magny-les-Villers
Corgoloin

"After rain comes rot then ruin." That succinctly sums up the pessimism deeply implanted in the Burgundian peasant, inherited from many generations of vineyard workers. It may also be why from time to time he may be heard murmuring the doleful words "Ca sent la merde." For indeed there are those who think the wines of Burgundy smell a bit like shit; or at least a whiff of the farmyard. What kept him at the beck and call of the soil? Because suffering, in one way or another in the end becomes endurable, and even acceptable. A French peasant 's life was hard and cruel; as their feudal system bit deeper and lasted longer than that which held the English peasantry in its thrall. Even long after the Revolution, the French farm worker clung to the land, so that even by 1945 more than 30% still worked it; against less than 10% in the UK. He was conservative, fought against change and was hostile to people outside of his commune; especially the absentee landowners either of the aristocracy or the Church. The weather was his unrelenting enemy; and as the local saying went "if our slopes were not the richest they'd be the poorest." So near did they live to the edge, and he was forever absorbed in the single task of feeding, housing and protecting his family from his natural enemies, landlords, landlords' agents, the Church and its agents; and the law such as it was.

It is not always realised that France was a divided country, and even now it is twice the area of the UK. It was divided into duchies that did not accept the King's authority, and the Dukes of Burgundy were the most powerful, the richest and had the largest army. The dukedom extended to what is now Belgium, the Netherlands, and the North East provinces of Flanders, Hainault and Picardy; plus a vast area between the Loire up to the mountains of the Jura in the east.

This geographical and political condition greatly influenced the people's character, and none more than the common people, so that they seemed like another race to the peasantry of the Bordeaux vineyards, part of Gascony, which also did not accept the French King's authority. Gascony was part of England, and the English played an enormous role in accentuating the differences which lasted nearly 300 years until the triumph of Joan of Arc at Orleans in 1453, when the English held territory, became part of France; as did Burgundy 25 years later. Another little known fact until well into the 18th century, there were 4 languages in France, each distinct from each other, and over 50 dialects.

The Phoenicians and the Greeks brought the vine to the southern parts of what is now France. Firstly around Marseilles and the Rhône estuary, and relatively north and east to the Midi and Provence. But it was the Romans with their usual speed that took viticulture, using the navigable advantages of the rivers, as far north as Dijon by the 2nd century. Italian merchants (trade always follows the flag) showed admirable enterprise in establishing entrepôts and offices around Lyons particularly for the export of wine to Italy. Wine would come by the Saône and Rhône rivers to Vienne near to Lyons. Vienne wines were as famous in the 2nd century as those of the Medoc are today. It is only the small area (150 acres) of the Côte Rhône, which denies its excellent red wines to most of Europe, and Vienne is its capital.

The Romans then established control of wine throughout the Empire using a pair of merchant associations, the "negotiatores vini supernates" using territory up to the Adriatic Ports and the "negotiatores vini internate" serving the Eastern Mediterranean. Such authority influenced what vines would be grown where; adopting for example, the Syrah to the northern Côte du Rhône; the Pinot Noir whose delicacy, acidity and finesse would have been dumbed-down by the powerful sun of the Rhône, was found to flourish further north on the current Côte d'Or; and the Pinot Noir has never done well outside of that area except in the Champagne where it provides as much as 70% of the grape content of Champagne. The Gamay grape which makes Beaujolais was banned in 1395 by Philip the Bold who was Duke at that time and referred to it as the "disloyal Gaamez, which gives wine in abundance but full of very great and horrible hardness." Inferior grapes introduced into a fine wine area produce an abundance of poor quality fruit. Yet the Gamay in the Beaujolais makes a pleasant wine of no great distinction, though nowhere else save Anjou where, when blended with Cabernet Franc makes a passable rosé. The cognoscenti of wine invariably refer to the Gamay grape as "indifferent", and they are right.

The majority, maybe 70% of the great reds are grown on the Côte de Nuits to the north of the Côte de Beaune which, in addition to many fine reds, is the principal home of the chardonnay grape which makes such splendid white wines whose greatness can be reached for by other growers of the grape but never grasped. The tiny village of Puligny-Montrachet from its small clos offers such splendid names as Les Pucelles, Le Chevalier Montrachet and Le Bâtard Montrachet.

All their splendour from a space not much more than 20 miles long and at its widest 1½ miles, which gave the name of Burgundy to the world. Though it produces but a fraction of the volume of wine, which comes out of that geographical area that is called "Burgundy". When the true wine lovers of the world talk about Burgundy, and if they are of the tiny minority that can afford it, they mean the wines of the Côte d'Or. Why, in the question of renown, these wines should be as famous as those of the Medoc, itself not a huge producer, is a mystery. Claret *and* Burgundy are synonymous with quality. Not, I fear that Burgundy in absolute terms is the equal, but the market, that mysterious something has largely decided that it is. If the wine of that tiny area, with its miniscule vineyards are sometimes superb it is *despite* the terrible vicissitudes that are rarely absent for more than a harvest or two. Too often the wines pick up insufficient colour and wines of a deeper red are added. There are hot summers but also cold winters, hard frosts. This does not matter, as winter provides the necessary dormancy the vine requires. It is the late frosts in April or May, which kill the fruit buds and thus much of the harvest. Rain and hail at critical periods of growth; insufficient September sun reduces the grape sugar which provides the alcohol. If the alcohol level is less than 11%, then cane sugar must be added to reach an alcohol level during fermentation of 11% to 12%. This process is called chaptalisation after its inventor, Jean Chaptal, and allowed by law up to a certain percentage of addition. You will not be surprised that sugar addition is often exceeded. On top of the weather problems is the grape. Only Pinot Noir is allowed, which is delicate, low yield and capricious. So the vigneron had no other grape to fall back on. Unlike in the Medoc where the great growths were a blend of Cabernet Sauvignon, Merlot and Malbec. Thus the peasant grower/owner/wine-maker (sometimes the same man), is often deeply in the merde and desperate to find a harvest from somewhere to have wine to sell and put food on his family's table. From all this it would be surprising if hypocrisy and law breaking did not take place and at the highest level despite the fact that over-sugaring causes that lack of balance which is the distinguishing feature of a great wine; and a combination of both headache and bellyache may follow. Heavy sugaring is an installed policy that is practised by estates both distinguished and lowly. Everybody is part of what is a widely recognised plot, growers, brokers, merchants and even customers. Ironically it was the growth of estate bottling, the growers answer to the rich, deep red velvety Mediterranean blends sold as Burgundy, which formed the public's palate, notably the British palate. And it was the wealthy English of the 18th and 19th centuries who wanted a Burgundy which under normal circumstances made a superb wine, quite different to what they, the English, wanted a Burgundy to be; and the customers, especially your best customer is always right, isn't he?

The troubles of the Burgundian grower may not be of the magnitude of those suffered by Job, but 10 harvest failures or part failure between 1961 and 1981 should be a burden too heavy to be borne. So the desperate grower against his wishes no doubt used his head to save his crop, with the aid of robust reds from the deep south loaded with alcohol, from the Midi, the Langedoc; and sometimes in abject desperation, from Algeria. The wine growers, like the foot soldier is at the sharp and dangerous end of the game. He seems to have been on his own, receiving very little support from either merchant, shipper or broker, who seemed to have taken the decision of a passive role. But when fermentation is finished, many tasks remain if a sound wine is to become available for retail sale. Moreover these tasks are those with which the growers had neither the skill or the desire to do, blending, chaptalising, ageing and bottling. And it was not until this work was largely taken over by the merchants and shippers, who had the capital or access to capital, so that sound reliable wines could be brought to market. For better or worse those who lived beyond the vineyard were the true guardians of what ended-up in the bottle. Responsible, in fact, for saying "This is a Le Corton, a Pommard a Flagey-Echézeaux, or a Romanée Conti" and without blinking an eyelid. It is probable that the changes that needed to be done have been done but up to at least 25 years ago, the state of wine at the quality end of the market was fragile. The whole affair in the matter of Grands Crus had become too *market responsible* for creating sales larger than the harvest, and that could only be done by doctoring the wine. If a wine was, or is, to become a "vin de garde", a wine for laying down, to benefit from maturation, then the desperate practices forced on the grower needed to be in skilled hands.

Where, might one ask, does that leave the wealthy, regular drinkers of highly priced reds from the Côte d'Or, or connoisseurs and the writers. This I must say is puzzling. It is possible that from time to time that a person whose reputation depends upon it cannot tell which wine is a Volnay and which a Grands Echézeaux? Though the same man (it is usually a man) can say with certitude that the wine he has just tasted is *not* a Lafite but an Haut-Brion both from the Medoc, though he will also say that the Haut-Brion is actually in Graves.

After giving a view or two about the Burgundy Côtes, which are not dissimilar to those held by people much more knowledgeable than me, it is useful to refer to that marvellous book by Michael Broadbent "The Great Vintage Wine Book." His judgements on Burgundies are as respected as his on Clarets; by me as well as most others. The book contains 873 tastings made between May 1967 and November 1979. I counted them. Now Burgundies, I thought, are not expected to make old bones, yet he wrote the following:-

> CHASSAGNE ROUGE 1832. Tired Strained old
> bouquet, slightly too acid but drinkable.

CORTON 1865. My first experience of a pre-phylloxera Burgundy. Fabulous old Pinot bouquet; a revelation.

CLOS VOUGEOT 1887. A delightful wine, sweet bouquet. Dry firm edge and finish.

BONNE MARES 1915. Beautiful rich old Pinot bouquet. Extremely attractive.

ROMANÉE CONTÉ 1929. Obviously thinner than in its youth but preserved by good tannin and acidity.

LE CHAMBERTIN 1949. A most beautiful ruddy mature colour. Nice but disappointing.

ROMANÉE ST VIVANT 1949. Fine deep fabulous almost exotic bouquet. Burgundy approaching its very best.

RICHEBOURG 1961. Very rich and most attractive bouquet. Great style and quality.

All of these were at least 10 years old and some of course very much older when tasted. Yet in my ignorance I thought Burgundies incapable of great ageing without losing all the original qualities. These 873 tastings represent a formidable performance; and I can only wonder that whatever the crafty desperate old Burgundian vigneron did to his wine, he mostly gave satisfaction and pleasure to the master taster, Michael Broadbent.

James Thurber could never have said of any of Mr Broadbent's tastings. "It's a naïve domestic Burgundy, but I think you will be amused by its presumption."

# 5

# SHERRY AND THE PROVINCE OF JEREZ

Spain, even today, is something of an enigma. With the death of Franco in 1975 the country seemed to leap from the 19th to the 20th century in weeks. Suddenly the girls were riding astride the back seats of boys' scooters instead of the demure side-saddle position as ordered by the authoritative Fascist regime; and smoking like chimneys. While the rest of Europe had rapidly industrialised since 1800–1850, Spain had resolutely resisted change; and as a consequence remained desperately poor, and none poorer than Andalusia, the home of sherry and of the grapes from which it is made. The Romans penetrated from 206BC, and it would have been out of character had their agronomists not brought the vine with them since they had planted in Gaul 200 years earlier. Moreover those great sea traders the Phoenicians in or around 500BC were in the area on their way to Britain for tin and although there is no evidence that they established settlements, they were great wine drinkers, and may well have planted. So wine as a crop was well established when the Islamic warriors from Morocco invaded "al-Andalus" as they called Spain; the land of the Vandals, in 710. The point of penetration was just around the corner from Jerez. During the more than 700 years that the Muslims were in Spain, wine making was not seriously impeded, despite the Islamic strictures against alcohol. The long period of occupation brought a measure of civilisation they had not known,

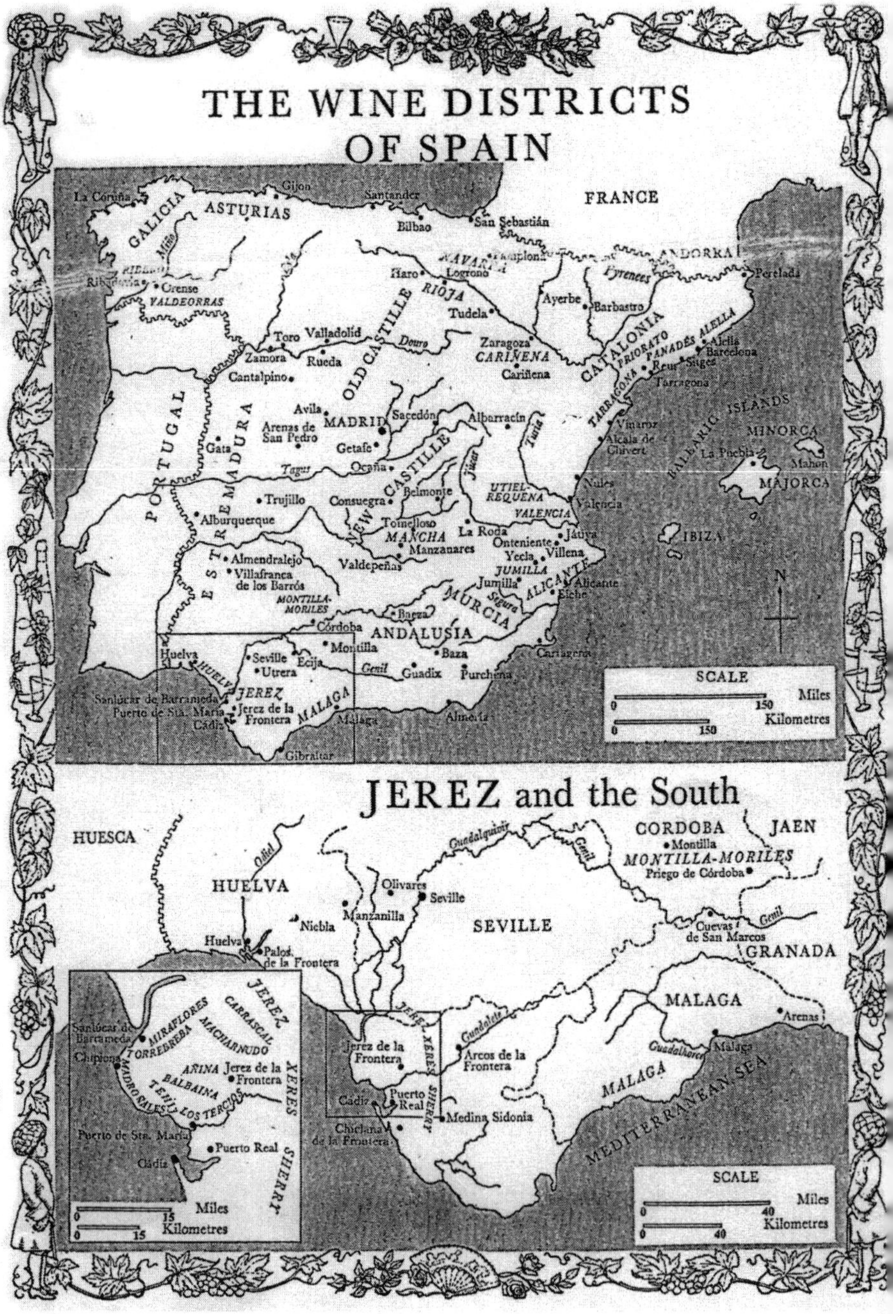
THE WINE DISTRICTS OF SPAIN
FRANCE
ANDORRA
Pyrenees
GALICIA
ASTURIAS
La Coruña
Gijon
Santander
Bilbao
San Sebastián
Orense
VALDEORRAS
NAVARRA
Haro
Logroño
RIOJA
Tudela
Ayerbe
Barbastro
Perelada
CATALONIA
PRIORATO
PANADÉS
ALELLA
Alella
Barcelona
Reus
Sitges
Tarragona
TARRAGONA
Zaragoza
CARIÑENA
Cariñena
Toro
Valladolid
Douro
Zamora
Rueda
OLD CASTILLE
Cantalpino
PORTUGAL
Avila
MADRID
Arenas de San Pedro
Getafe
Sacedón
Albarracín
Gata
ESTREMADURA
Tagus
Ocaña
NEW CASTILLE
Belmonte
Turia
Júcar
UTIEL-REQUENA
VALENCIA
Valencia
Vinaroz
Alcala de Chivert
Nules
BALEARIC ISLANDS
MINORCA
Mahon
La Puebla
MAJORCA
IBIZA
Trujillo
Consuegra
Alburquerque
Tomelloso
MANCHA
Manzanares
La Roda
Onteniente
Játiva
Yecla
Villena
JUMILLA
Jumilla
Almendralejo
Villafranca de los Barros
Valdepeñas
MONTILLA-MORILES
MURCIA
Segura
ALICANTE
Alicante
Elche
Baeza
Córdoba
ANDALUSIA
Montilla
Baza
Huelva
HUELVA
Seville
Ecija
Utrera
Genil
Guadix
Purchena
Cartagena
N
JEREZ
Sanlúcar de Barrameda
Puerto de Sta. María
Jerez de la Frontera
Cádiz
MALAGA
Málaga
Almeria
Gibraltar
SCALE
Miles
Kilometres
0
150
JEREZ and the South
HUESCA
CORDOBA
JAEN
Montilla
MONTILLA-MORILES
Priego de Córdoba
Guadalquivir
Genil
HUELVA
Odiel
Olivares
Seville
Manzanilla
Niebla
SEVILLE
Cuevas de San Marcos
GRANADA
Huelva
Palos de la Frontera
JEREZ
CARRASCAL
MIRAFLORES
MACHARNUDO
TORREBREBA
Sanlúcar de Barrameda
Chipiona
AÑINA
Jerez de la Frontera
BALBAINA
MADROÑALES
TEHIGO
LOS TERCIOS
XERES
SHERRY
Puerto de Sta. María
Puerto Real
Cádiz
Miles
Kilometres
0
15
MALAGA
Arenas
Málaga
Guadalhorce
Guadalete
Jerez de la Frontera
Arcos de la Frontera
Cádiz
Puerto Real
Medina Sidonia
Chiclana de la Frontera
MALAGA
MEDITERRANEAN SEA
SCALE
Miles
Kilometres
0
40

in architecture, art, philosophy, in medicine and in agriculture. This was at a time when Europe as a whole, including, and especially England had hardly moved on from the Dark Ages. Jerez, and the nearby ports of El Puerto de Santa Maria and San Lucar de Barrameda benefited mightily and became sizeable ports and towns for export/import trades based on wine and fruit. With the final departure of the Muslim rulers in 1492, and the expulsion of the Jews also, just to show how even handed they were, the Church established its firm grip again and the clock of civilised advancement stopped. In 1951 when the Atlee Social Government was replaced by the Conservatives, Evelyn Waugh was moved to say later "The Tories have been in power for 6 months and they have not put the clock back by a single minute." Waugh was a convert to Catholicism, and was as they say "one of the old school."

With the expulsion of the Jews and other heretics after 1492 especially in such ports as Cadiz, the vacuum caused by the departure was gradually filled by the likes of Genoese, some Dutch and Germans, but in particular men from the British Isles. Jerez with its ports on the River Guadalete seemed to act like a honey pot. A further boost to the areas importance came when Columbus sailed from Sanlucar de Barrameda on his 3rd voyage of exploration to the West Indies, which was established as a major port for the American trade. From that time Jerez became well known as a wine grower and exporter of wine; although there is evidence that England imported wine from Cadiz during the reign of Edward III when the Moors were still in power. So in many ways the stage for the advent much later of the English, Anglo Irish, Celtic Irish and Scottish Catholic merchant adventurers was set *before* Spain freed itself from the rule of the Islamic heretics. The Dukes of Medina Sidonia were clearly early Anglophiles, and encouraged English merchants to settle, and granted them substantial privileges; which included the generous gift of land on which to build a church dedicated to St George. This, of course, was before Henry VIII had his little tiff with Rome.

The nature of Andalusian wines of this time is anybody's guess. As a still, natural wine, it must have been powerful stuff. The must, produced under the powerful sun probably gave a fermentation of 13%–15% alcohol; strong enough even for the English but *was* distilled alcohol also added? Distillation was an ancient Egyptian discovery (or was it the Chinese?), so the Moors would have known how to do it. So also would the conquered Spanish. Whatever its make-up it was generally known as sherry, or earlier, sherry sack especially by the English, and it is an historical fact that by the early 16th century, many of them, gentlemen of leisure had settled in the agreeable climate around Jerez. By Henry VIII's time there were so many that a petition to him granted them the right to form a constitution, and they called themselves the Andalusian Company. Naturally they formed a Club; the English Club, though it took a generation or two before the HP Sauce, Marmite and Wall's Sausages were available. The Andalusian Company also called the Brotherhood of St George, must have been the first of a long line of Ex-pats clubs. A refuge to which the British who, after a day's work could cut themselves off from the Foreigner for a few hours; where neither religion nor politics was discussed. Trade followed the flag and after trade the Club, which could be a temple of seclusion and magnificence. The grandest, old India hands would say was the Bengal Club in Calcutta. Though for me my vote goes to the Gezira in Cairo. It was outrageous in its opulence and exclusivity; with its race course, Polo field, cricket ground, croquet lawns, swimming pools, restaurant and accommodation, and for what? 400 cavalry officers.

So the stage was set for the Anglo Saxon invasion during the 18th, 19th and early 20th centuries; and there are a number of significant causes. There are 5 dates, which fairly accurately establish the flight of the Irish, particular the Norman/English, and the Celtic Irish. They fled Ireland to escape the vengeance of the English, and invariably halted in Spain or France; feeling secure among fellow Catholics. The dates were 1607, 1641–50, 1690, 1798. Earlier there was a flight of Catholics from Scotland after the disastrous battle of Culloden in 1746, at which they gave brave but futile support to Bonny Prince Charlie in his attempt to claim the English Throne. The punishments inflicted on those who stayed in Scotland were outstandingly cruel, and the '45 Rebellion, as it was called still has resonance in the Highlands from whence most of the Catholics came.

Hugh O'Neall brought up by the powerful Sydney family in Penshurst, Kent, was rescued from the warring factions in Ulster at the age of nine. The O'Neall's were at war with each other disputing the Earldom of Tyrone. Sir Philip Sydney, looking far ahead, thought the boy could in a few years be taught to be an English gentleman, skilled in statecraft and government, and in time returned to Ulster to pacify the O'Neall's and others, as the Earl of Tyrone. Had Sydney been able to foresee the future, he would have had the boy quietly strangled. As it was, he was returned to Ireland at the age of 16; and he took as his first task of hunting out those who had murdered his father, any of his cousins he could find; and put them to the sword or worse, less they prevented his appointment by the English as the 4th Earl of Tyrone in 1587. He then set out to remove the English, not only from Ulster but also from the other 3 provinces of Ireland, Munster, Leinster and Connaught and in the ensuing years he damn near succeeded. Taking advantage of his English upbringing particularly in the study of the art of warfare, he inflicted such defeats and casualties on the standing English army that Elizabeth had to send a further 30,000 soldiers to deal with Hugh. He became the greatest political and military leader ever produced by Ireland. In the end the task was too great and the O'Neall's, along with the Earl of Tyrconnel, their families and all their retainers, quit Ireland in 1607 in what became known as the Flight of the Earls. Descendents of Hugh and the others live and prosper in Spain today; and there were regular arrivals from Ireland in the 17th, 18th and 19th centuries to form and continually be recruited into the Irish Brigades in the various Continental Armies which fought against the British. They were known as "The Wild Geese".

Hugh O'Neall is generally regarded as an early Anglo-Irishman.

Ireland was perpetually at war from 1641 to 1650, when at great and bloody cost, Oliver Cromwell came over with his professional army and pacified the country, killing Irish Catholics and English Catholics even-handedly, but brought a peace that lasted until 1690 when King William came over to defeat the dethroned James II at the Battle of the Boyne. From 1641 until after the Boyne there was a steady flow of Irish to Spain and France. Then in 1798 the great '98 Rebellion started and it was the greatest uprising Ireland had known for nearly 200 years. It was different to other outbreaks because for the first time Protestants joined with Catholics in a serious attempt to persuade England to surrender authority, and allow the Irish to rule themselves. It failed bloodily and many more fled to Europe, particularly from among the Irish gentry.

A typical émigré was Rafael O'Neale (note the name change from the Celtic). He and a relative, Timothy O'Neale, established his bodega in Jerez in 1724. Later many of the Gordon clan, along with other Scottish Catholics fled their ancient homes after Culloden to end-up in Spain, and intermarried with Spanish families in the sherry trade. One of these was Gonzalez, who even changed its name to Gonzalez-Gordon.

There is a well recorded history of English, Irish and Scottish ex-patriots in Spain; and at least 120 were involved in some way with the growing, blending, shipping or selling sherry; not only to the UK but to much of the world. The Spanish marriages were blessed with many children to increase the ex-patriot tribes in that small area known as Sherry Country. Few people who have drunk a bottle or two will not be unfamiliar with the town of Jerez de la Frontera, which is synonymous with sherry. Only nine miles from the sea between Cadiz and Seville, it is the most important of three towns that make the world's sherry. The others are El Puerto de Santa Maria, and San Lucar de Barrameda. The area seems ridiculously small to contain the reputation its wine has held for centuries.

Where sherry country seems different from, for example, Bordeaux is, or at any rate was, the almost total barrier between the peasantry who tended the vines and the minor gentry (usually Spanish) and the ex-patriot merchants who put together the finished product and shipped it. Even the vineyard toilers rarely lived on the job. There were few dwellings among the vines; maybe a shack or two for use during harvest time; the peasant preferring the safety of his village to the frequent dangers of the open country where brigandry caused by severe poverty was constantly present. Andalusia and the neighbouring province of Estramadura were, up until the Civil War of 1936–39 with its over a million dead, the poorest people in Europe. I recall motoring through the area about my business in the years from 1950 until at least 1970, observing a deprived yet proud people still suffering from the horrors of war. The sherry towns were where the wines after fermentation were taken. More often than not beginning in the early 20thy century the grapes must were taken to the towns *before* fermentation; thus divorcing even more the growing from the making. During the 19th century the landowners built comfortable, well appointed houses on their vineyards which they might occupy during the Summer, but there was nothing of the intimacy between owner and peasant that was normal in Bordeaux, where the owner had his permanent dwelling amidst his vineyards while his workers lived in the village of which the vincyards were a part.

Attempts had been made by an organisation called the Wine Growers Guild, known as the GREMIO, which tried to fix the price of the grapes and the must. Growers were not allowed to be merchants and the merchants were not allowed to build up large stocks of wine. The GREMIO was a typical bureaucratic attempt to interfere with free trade and competition and in the long-run was bound to fail. It was a *very* long run; 101 years, and when it was dissolved in 1834, it could look back on a long life of severe damage to the sherry trade. Thereafter the big shippers were able to build-up large stocks of old wines to blend into regular and balanced sherries.

Before the shippers and merchants appeared on the scene, the peasant grower who rarely had a financial stake in the wine making business would grow and dress the vines, pick the grapes and press them by foot, carry out the fermentation, store the finished wine in vessels of some sort;

barrels if they had any, and sell from the barrel early in the year after harvest. But the merchant would buy the grapes, bring them to his property on which he had built his bodega, the special above-ground structure in which the wine would be made, from pressing to fermentation to blending by what came to be known as the "solera system". So out of the primitive peasant practice, emerged firstly the destructive interference of the GREMIO which led to the merchant driven modern practice based on huge stocks of wine, controlled blending and the availability, nationwide and worldwide of seamless, drinkable sherries.

The bodega is what gives a lot of style to Jerez, a pleasant but otherwise undistinguished town. An earlier travel writer named Richard Ford, who wrote "Handbook for Travellers in Spain", thought that bodegas had much in common with cathedrals. A difficult simile perhaps, but both can be permeated with sunlight, though a bodega at the same time is also permeated with the smell, the heavy aroma of maturing wine. Some, though not all cathedrals can be awesome, so can some bodegas; through their height, breadth, length, but mainly through the vast volume of wine contained therein.

The basic design in bodega construction was taken-up by the merchants and often built adjacent to the house; so beautiful, often with lovely gardens, they could be described almost as a fashion accessory to a rich merchant's house. Although the system built bodega dates from the mid-19th century they continue to be built. Crofts built Rancho Croft in 1970, and Domecq built, at the same time, one inspired by the Great Mosque in Cordoba. Another acknowledgement of the architectural skills of Spain's Muslim conquerors.

If there ever was a single person who conceived the basic idea of the modern bodega, then his name does not seem to have been recorded, but the design seems faithful to an original idea; aesthetically pleasing and of a distinctive school of architecture. The Spanish had a reputation for constructing not only buildings of good design but also of enduring life. Never more so than in the building of frigates and battle cruisers. The Royal Navy was always pleased to capture a Spanish vessel because it tended to be superior to anything coming out of the Royal shipyards at Deptford, Greenwich or Chatham. Maybe the Spanish had their labour under better financial control than that which ruled in the British yards where corruption was the order of the day. Even Samuel Pepys, the Naval Secretary, failed to deal with the corruption. In the end he gave-up, joined-in and became very rich.

The bodega needs to be cool in Summer, but far from freezing in Winter. So the walls are thick and made with hollow bricks; air is a good insulator. The roofs are insulated with sheets of cork and the circulation of air, so necessary to wine stability is added to by many small windows protected by grills. These could be covered with blinds in Summer to keep the temperature down. It is likely that the originator of bodega construction was influenced by the Muslim conquerors who, coming from the Middle East with its extremes of temperatures, knew from hundreds of years of experience how to keep cool in Summer and warm in Winter.

Sherry making requires the bodega to make possible the creation of the solera, the method of blending a series of wines of different years into a sherry which will remain stable in quality, colour and of recognisable character over the years. The temperature should never be too cold as this can cause cream of tartar to be precipitated out of solution. This makes the wine cloudy and it must be filtered before shipping.

The solera is a strange structure. In charge is the Capataz, who carries out the work of the Maître de Chai in a Medoc winery, and chooses the butts of young wines of similar styles but of varying years. The bottom line of butts is called the solera, from which wine is drawn for bottling or sale in barrel. Above the solera are perhaps as many as 6 lines of butts called criaderas, with the youngest wines at the top. This layout allows wines to be siphoned progressively over a period of months from the top row into the solera at the bottom. The system must be constructed with great care, for the weights involved are enormous; and should a butt be displaced the structure could collapse. Thus are the young wines added to the bottom row of old wine to form the blend, and the process is repeated under the guidance of the Capataz. The system is remarkable in maintaining the unchanging nature of the old wine, which will be tapped for shipment. The solera system is the reason why bottles of sherry do not show a vintage year. There is no such thing as a vintage sherry.

It is highly improbable that Spain had much of an export wine trade before Ferdinand of Aragon and Isabella of Cadiz, joint rulers of that part of Spain not conquered by the Muslims, completed the re-conquest in 1492. Spain then enjoyed its "golden age" and under their rule a great empire grew which included most of the West Indies, the whole of Central America, Mexico, much of the New World, Cuba, Peru, the Canary Islands and the Philippines. All empires in the end break-up. The Spanish was no different to the others, and by the early 19th century decay and dissolution was all but complete. But trade had developed and continued in the colonies and former colonies all of which were a larger market for wine and other vinous products. There is evidence that exports to England date from at least the time of

Edward III, in the middle of the 14th century but it would have been sporadic and of uneven quality. Undoubtedly great changes, though inimical to the Catholic Church, started from the time the first merchant adventures set foot in Cadiz and Puerto de Santa Maria. Mostly they came from Ireland, Scotland and England, but also from Holland and Germany. Apart from the Catholics who were political refugees, there were not a few Protestants, a strange paradox bearing in mind the intolerant, puritanical nature of Spanish Catholicism. The Protestants brought with them many skills; technical, managerial, engineering and entrepreneurial, learnt in the hard business climate of Northern Europe, where failure led to bankruptcy and success richly rewarded. Some married into Spanish land-owning and merchant families, to the great benefit of most; and the descendants of those who took the frequently dangerous decision to establish themselves in Spain are many, and still in the sherry trade. Their stories may vary from the tragic to the comic; but few lacked interest and eccentrics abounded to an unusual degree.

# 6

## THE EXPATRIATES & OTHERS

**BURDON** John William worked as a clerk in Duff Gordon Company. This status of employee thought not uncommon suggests he did not venture into Spain "on spec" as it were, but was probably recruited in London by the Duff Gordon Family. In any case clearly he was ambitious and able, and before long he decided to quit Duff Gordon, and set-up on his own. Within a few years he had built-up a highly successful business; buying the firm of Harmony in 1840, and married a Señora Carmen Berges. By 1854 Burdon was the leading shipper, followed by Garvey. There were no children of the marriage, and the company was sold, firstly to Luis de la Cuesta, and secondly to Luis Caballero in 1932 who expanded the company and built a beautiful bodega in El Puerta de Santa Maria with lovely gardens. The Burdon name continued as a separate marque for a long time, and Burdon was the best example of an ex-pat. A credit to the country from which he emigrated and to Spain where he lived and prospered. Caballero kept all Burdon's accounts and many of his letters dating back to the early part of the 19th century, a great contribution to the social history of the time.

**DOMECQ** Pedro. The Domecq's were not of course ex-patriots from Great Britain but they were so much involved with them through marriage and business, that by the time José Ignacio Domecq died at 83 in 1997, he probably had as much English, Scottish and Irish blood in him as Spanish. It will surprise many that the family business was founded by an Irishman, Patrick Murphy, a winegrower (as he is described) in 1730. He had a close friend, Juan Haurie, who helped in the management of his vineyards. Haurie, on Patrick's death, was the sole inheritor of his vineyards, his properties, and anything that had been his in Spain; and the vineyards were in the best areas of Jerez. Like Murphy, and in the less than subtle language of Private Eye Magazine, he was a confirmed bachelor but he had 5 nephews whom he brought into the business. One of them, Pedro Lembeye, son of Haurie's sister Doña Maria, had a sister who married a Domecq and gave birth to Pedro.

The Peninsular War destroyed many people and many businesses. Particularly vulnerable were those who had favoured the French, thinking Napoleon's genius would give them victory. Juan Carlos, last of the 5 nephews, was a Spaniard who became a major supplier of food and drink to the French Army. This was his undoing and led ultimately to his humiliating bankruptcy, most of the vineyards, bodegas and wine went to Pedro Domecq and by 1821 he was trading under his own name, though the sherry trade was in poor shape, as was most of Spain when the French departed; chivvied all the way to Toulouse in 1814 by Sir Arthur Wellesley and his British soldiers. It took a man resolute, far seeing and hard working to restore sherry and Pedro was that man; but let it not be forgotten that without the Irish bachelor, Patrick Murphy, the name of Domecq might only have been that of a minor player in Jerez.

Much of Pedro's early education and work experience was in England, so he was in a good place to take on board Northern Protestant hard-nosed business practices. He deliberately chose to work as a clerk in the London Office of Haurie's agents Gordon, Murphy & Co., which gave him a sound background in the wine trade, particularly in selling. While in London he married Diana Lancaster of Bermondsey and 5 daughters gave a firm base to the future Domecq dynasty. He once claimed to have made a fortune in 2 years of hard work. Tragically he was killed in February 1839. Suffering badly from rheumatism, he was advised steam treatment, for which he was suspended over a large cauldron of boiling water. The structure collapsed, he fell into the cauldron and died a few days later from massive burns; he was 57. His estate yielded over one million pounds, a vast fortune for the times, and as he grew rich he drew a large handful of others especially well known Anglo Saxons into the tight circle of the wealthy. Pedro made certain that henceforth until the present day every Domecq would know from whence the next meal was coming. From that time also the foreign colony grew in strength and numbers, and the most prosperous shippers, merchants and growers were numbered among the English, Scots and the Irish.

These wealthy sherry families knew the meaning of the mantra "critical mass" before it was invented by the Massachusetts Institute of Technology, the first of the great business schools. Domecq knew that survival depended on size, and they swallowed minnows, smaller growers and shippers; but big as they grew, others grew bigger and they agreed to become part of Allied Lyons and then Allied Domecq. This preserved both name and fortune, but only one significant family member remained with the multinational. Most of the others, proud people stayed in Spain, still independent and still making sherry. One of them, Alvaro Domecq, had been a "rejoneador" a fighter of bulls on horseback. This was the old way of bull fighting; and when he became too old for this dangerous pursuit he became a breeder of fighting bulls. He also bought an "almacenista", the name given to a small blender and trader, from Pilar Aranda, who had been a sherry maker since 1800. Several others took the same route of buying small independent blenders.

The Domecqs' had style but they never let hubris or flashiness interfere with the prime object, which was making a success of wine growing and sherry making. When José Ignacio Domecq died in 1997 of lung cancer at 83, he was the last of the line of great sherry makers. Known as El Nariz "The Nose", which was an arresting sight, and was said to have made him a great blender of superb sherry. He was equally good at creating large families; and of his seven sons and five daughters, doubtless some of them, or their families, are still keeping the Domecq name in the news.

He was a great Anglophile, and it would be surprising if his hats were not made by Lock of St James Street; his suits perhaps built (one can use no other word) by Gieves and Hawkes of Saville Row; his shirts made by Turnbull and Asser and his shoes by Mr Lobb, both of Jermyn Street.

**DUFF** Sir James was the type of man that gave character and probity both to his business and private life. Born in Ayrshire in 1734 he was British Consul at Cadiz in the second half of the 18th century. In those days a Consul was an unpaid representative of the local British community and his major duty lay in acting for the British Government in matters that concerned merchants that got into trouble with local law and national authorities. If he was a strong character of a persuasive and diplomatic disposition his value in defence of his countrymen was priceless. Sir James was of that kind. If the office was unpaid the Consul was usually involved in trade in his case wines, which he was certainly buying and shipping-out before 1770. The Spanish liked him and his support and activity during the Peninsular War earned him his baronetcy. There is no evidence that he did other than buy wine from the Franco/Spanish firm of Juan Haurie. That is he neither grew, fermented nor blended. But by 1818, (he died in 1815 just in time to hear of Wellington's victory at Waterloo), his successors had built-up a large market in England, at high prices to the Prince Regent and his disreputable friends.

Sir James left his sherry business to his kinsman, Sir William Duff Gordon, who saw no great virtue in hard work, and was not overburdened in the brain department. He was MP for Worcester and spent money as a Regency Buck was expected to do, wastefully. A small fortune on contesting elections, £20,000 on a house in Portland Place and £10,000 on jewels when he married. Whether the jewels were for him or his wife is not recorded. Any contributions he made to the business were largely nugatory, if not failures; and in the end he withdrew from it, leaving it to the professionals, and the Duff Gordon family interests continued by Cosmo Duff Gordon prospered, and sherry was sold under the Duff Gordon name until 1890.

**GARVEY** William was born in New Ross in County Waterford, came to Spain in 1780 and became a general merchant in San Lucar de Barrameda, a port on the River Guadalquiver. Vineyards in the area grow the grapes from which is made Manzanilla, a fino of such astounding dryness that those bearing the well known fino names of Tio Pepé and La Ina taste almost sweet. A manzanilla is for hardened sherry topers. Apart from wines Garvey sold, of all things, snuff. He must have made up his mind to go native when he married a Spanish girl in 1794 and so sherry became his business. He was a kinsman of the Dukes of Ormonde, the

Butler family who came over to Ireland during the reign of King John. Along with the Dukes of Desmond, the Fitzgeralds, they were the two great Norman/Irish families, and what the Butlers didn't own the Fitzgeralds usually did. Both were nominally Catholic, but when it was politically incorrect to be Catholic, ie. when the English Monarch got snotty-nosed about it, they were always ready to embrace the Heretical Protestant God of the English in order to keep their lands and wealth.

William Garvey was probably equally casual and slipped back into smells and bells to marry into a Spanish family.

He built a huge bodega, at the time there was none bigger in Jerez. It measured 558 feet long x 126 feet wide and very high; a veritable cathedral, and stylish. To feed his bodega he bought a lot of his wine from the Gordon family, and from Bernard Shiel another Irishman. Shiel, a good grower, was better known as one of four foreigners who did a lot to mitigate the horrors of cholera, which in 1834 swept through the area. Four thousand died in 3 months. Instead of prayer as advocated by the Spanish authorities, they visited the fever-ridden quarters of the town preaching the virtues of clean drinking water, personal hygiene and ventilation.

Streetwise and a good businessman, Garvey made a superb fino and called it St Patricio after his patron saint and it is still made. William Garvey was an archetypal Anglo Irishman whose principal interests were women, drink and horses, which he bred in his own stud and which produced winners all over Europe.

**GORDON** Arthur came from Scotland in 1756 or maybe earlier. He was the younger brother of the Laird of Beldorney and came over to become a merchant in Cadiz. In 1774 he bought his own bodega in Jerez and by 1800 had become a leading blender and a prominent member of the British community. A devout Catholic, in his will, when he died in 1815 he had left a substantial legacy to the Scotch College in Valladolid. Leaving no son, his kinsman, Charles Peter Gordon inherited; his many descendants still live in Jerez, active in the sherry trade today. Some married into the Gonzalez family, which changed its name to Gonzalez-Gordon; Others into Domecqs.

Charles Peter was popular and his bodega visited by many British visitors who enjoyed his lavish hospitality. He had a son, also C P Gordon, who had been appointed Consul at Cadiz, and was as bigoted a Catholic in Cadiz as Dr Ian Paisley is a bigoted Protestant in Ulster. So monolithic was his Catholicism he could not bear to have a Protestant, laity or clergyman on the Consulate premises. And he cordially disliked his non-Catholic fellow ex-patriots also. Complaints to London followed and he was dismissed in 1861. But Gordon was obstinate and would not part either with the official seal or with the archives and kept the British Coat of Arms above his house doorway. His successor was Charles Harman Furlong, whom Gordon set-out to discredit; accusing him of being a liberal, a paid agent of a secret religious society, and a distributor of Protestant bibles. Many of the sherry trade were sorry to see Gordon go as he was the source of much amusement, particularly as Furlong turned out to be dishonest. C P Gordon was only one of a number of giddy eccentrics to emerge from the growing Gordon clan.

Now, sherry brings me to a strange story that started on the battlefield of Culloden in 1745, and ended with the death of a very old friend on the 22nd October 2002.

There was a family of Gordons, one of many Highland clans, which in the Jacobite Rebellion of 1745 elected to fight for the Young Pretender, Bonnie Prince Charlie. After the defeat at the Battle of Culloden in 1745 many of the Catholics of Scotland fled abroad to avoid capture, torture and almost certain execution in the nastiest possible way. Like most of the Highland clans they were Catholic recusants, refusing to recognise either the faux Protestant faith of Henry VIII or the Covenanters of Edinburgh. Finally in about 1780 this Gordon branch, or some of them, ended up in Jerez de la Frontera, planted vineyards, made fine sherries and prospered mightily. They intermarried with Domecq and Gonzales Biaz, the greatest of the sherry families. Finally a fair number of them, grandfathers, fathers, sons, daughters came back to the UK in 1905, and Louis' grandfather became the UK selling end of Domecq. By that time Spain had Gordons all over the sherry area, breeding prolifically as devout Catholics and, unlike Onan of Biblical notoriety, they spilt not their seed upon the ground. The Spanish Gordons are in Jerez today.

The family threw up a fair handful of eccentrics. One, Alexander Gordon, was publicly guillotined at Brest in 1769, supposedly as an English spy. Another, Juan José Gordon, went back to Woodhouse near Aberdeen as laird, as the Gordons had been for countless generations. At Woodhouse, he built a bullring, imported Spanish bulls, and invited his Spanish friends to Woodhouse to practise the ancient craft of tauromachy.

I first met Luiz George Anthony Maria Gordon, 20 years old and just married, in the George Hotel, Crawley, on a Saturday morning in 1954, a favourite watering hole of the Sussex jeunesse doré in those days. There were other Gordons alongside and Luiz and I hit it off immediately. He had just had his 21st birthday at which the pipe of port (110 gallons) laid down by his father on the day of his birth was broached. We met frequently thereafter until a few months before his death. He played the largest possible part in putting Domecq on the UK sherry map, and added a new dimension to corporate entertainment when he chartered a Comet aeroplane, filled it with journalists, publicans and wine traders and flew them down to Jerez. Luiz was no ordinary salesman. There, when they were drunk, he invited the guests to enter the ring and play with a bull or two.

In 1970 he bought a wine bar in Villiers Street alongside Charing Cross station. Coincidentally, it was called Gordon's Wine Bar, but no relation, that Gordon opened it in the 19th century and was the first in London. It is in a cellar, and was and is a dump, but Luiz would never, ever, remove a single cobweb or clean away any dust. It serves all the fortified wines from the barrel, the food is very decent, and it is always full. As they say, le tout monde would come to Luiz's Bar.

At the Memorial Service, many people could not get into the church, where they stood in the nave and the aisles. Luiz died on 22nd October 2002 AD, leaving six sons and Wendy, his wife. In 69 years he contributed greatly to the gaiety of life. Two weeks later Wendy threw a party at the wine bar and the cheerful boozers spilt out onto the pavement.

**HARVEY** John & Sons Ltd. The very house was synonymous with sherry. When you thought of sherry you thought of Harvey's; and when you thought of Harvey's you thought of Bristol Cream, the most famous sherry in the whole wide world; not the best, but the most famous. The blend was made from the three basic sherries: Fino, Amontillado and Oloroso, and John Harvey said the blend started with wines from fifty soleras; with some Pedro Ximinez to add sweetness. It is also claimed that with advantage it can be served chilled and on the rocks. The Americans would have liked that, and maybe why it outsells its nearest competitor in America by 2 to 1. It really *did* cut across the class barriers, which isolated the Fino and the dry Amontillado drinkers of the middle classes from the rest of us. A brilliant piece of marketing, and it made the family very wealthy. This marvellous coup was pulled off in the 1860's-1880's, and it continues to be a big seller. Moreover all this was done from their cellars and works in Bristol, and they did not own a bodega in Jerez or anywhere else until 1970.

The company actually began with William Perry who set-up a retail wine business in an old larger house in Denmark Street, Bristol. The year was 1796, and there were extensive cellars. An ideal starting point for a company that was to have a life of a family business for more than 200 years. Perry sold sherry and port and took Thomas Urch into partnership. Urch's sister Ann was the 2nd wife of Thomas Harvey of Bristol, a renowned sea captain. His son, the 2nd John Harvey, didn't fancy the sea as a career, and entered his Uncle Urch's wine business in 1822 at 16. When Perry died in 1820 he was made a partner, and in 1840 became the virtual owner of John Harvey & Sons Ltd., which was managed by successive generations of the Harvey family.

They were outstanding shippers and blenders for over 150 years; during which time they had hardly a need to step foot in Spain, buying wines direct from the oldest wine company in Jerez, Manuel Misa who shipped it to Bristol. It was not until 1970 when they bought Mackenzie and Company with their huge volume of fine wines and excellent bodega that they established a permanent company in Jerez. They then bought the Misa bodega with its beautiful gardens and gained what they had been after in Jerez, an extended blending capacity. But they were not finished yet, and in the late 1970's they purchased the Gibalbin Vineyards to guarantee their supply of wine. This was further evidence of their skill and strong determination to keep ahead of the game. By buying Mackenzie, the brilliant engineer and designer Diego Ferguson came with the deal. Though born in Jerez, he had studied wine making in South Africa and Australia, where he found that the traditional vertical press had been replaced by the horizontal press, which was continuous in operation instead of pressing in batches. Ferguson took the idea back to Spain, improved it and Harvey's inherited it.

They were outstandingly astute in keeping in market lead, and always had a sharp eye on new engineering and mechanical progress. Bottling wines both in Spain *and* France had always been primitive particularly in the matters of hygiene and general cleanliness; neglect of which will ruin a wine. Shippers took up bottling and established plants in London; and Harvey's also in Bristol for their sherries *and* Bordeaux wines. Even in the Medoc most of the great names preferred their wines to be bottled in England as late as the 1960's. There was, at Harvey's, an Englishman named George McWatters, who had been trained in Bordeaux and he set-up a school to train budding wine tasters and students of wine lore. Among his students was the young Michael Broadbent who had joined Harvey's in 1957 and later became head of Christie's London Wine Auction Rooms. There is nobody more respected in the world than Broadbent in the matter of Claret and Burgundy wines.

John Harveys were not expatriates in Spain but they were important members of the Jerez elite. Very early they exhibited that Anglo Saxon Protestant zeal in identifying where the best profit lay; deciding it was in buying, blending and selling direct to the wholesaler and retailer. But also where necessary owning the vineyards and blending both in Spain and in England. No company in the sherry business did it better and they were justly well rewarded.

**MACKENZIE** Kenneth came to Jerez in the mid-19th century and set-up as a buyer and shipper. The firm prospered as Mackenzie & Co., and in due course was inherited by Kenneth's nephew Peter. He, in the great tradition of the Anglo expatriate, was another eccentric. He ran the business well but though long domiciled in Spain, never managed to achieve even a modest fluency in the tongue and conversed to his Spanish friends in pigeon Spanish, which they greeted with howls of laughter. Like an acquaintance of mine who, with his brother, resisted vigorously his headmaster's attempt to teach them much in the way of reading, writing and arithmetic. This apparent self-taught ignorance in no way impeded their joint great success in business. It was more than a century later in 1970 that Harvey bought Mackenzie, a thriving company; and with it a fine bodega and a huge stock of wine such as Mackenzie had been selling to them for years. This gave Harvey's their first solid footing in Jerez, and now they would be blending in Spain as well as Bristol, but the name of Mackenzie continued despite being sold to Harvey's which ended-up in the multi-national Allied Domecq, sacrificed on the alter of critical mass.

**MURPHY** Patrick came to Jerez sometime before 1730. He grew wine, prospered, cared little for business and was unmarried. There are some contradictions here, positively oxymoronic. It is difficult to prosper without interest or skill in what you are doing; and if you grew wine either you bought a vineyard or you planted one. Both needed capital even in a country as poor as 18th century Spain. He died in 1762, leaving considerable property and vineyards to his friend, and probably lover, Juan Haurie, who was a general merchant, but not including wine until he started to help Murphy in 1745. After the Battle of the Boyne in 1690 there was peace in Ireland until the Uprising of 1798. So it is unlikely that Murphy left to avoid prison or religious persecution. Patrick Murphy was a Catholic name at a time when a man's religion was noted. He *must* have gone to Spain with money, yet in Ireland at that time to find anybody named Murphy with two pennies to rub together would not have been an every day event. There is some mystery surrounding that Irishman, and I fancy it must involve his friend Haurie, who did know the ins and outs of business, especially in Spain and he would have taught himself about viticulture and wine making soon enough. But what Haurie did have of very great value was an extended family of brothers, nephews and no doubt a few nieces. Murphy was not robust or in good health, and even somebody of a less suspicious nature than me might have considered first, gentle and then firmer pressure from the Haurie family "tout court" might have guided his quavering hand to the bottom of the last page of his Will. Haurie was French, a refugee, and he was joined in Spain by kinsmen, who worked in the wine trade. Linguistically, Patrick would have been outnumbered, could have used a good lawyer; a Jewish one for preference. Lacking this Haurie got all his property.

When Juan Haurie became the owner and in sole control, he appointed Gordon Murphy & Co., as English agents. They had 3 partners, Sir William Duff, James Farrell and Colonel Murphy. Was he a relative? Doubtful, as he would surely have contested Patrick's Will leaving everything to Haurie. Is there a sniff of conspiracy theory here? But it is all very mystifying and not solved when Pedro Domecq takes over a considerable sherry empire from the Hauries' who got it from a Catholic Irishman of no known abode in Ireland with the unfashionable name of Murphy.

**O'NEALE** Timothy. The O'Neale's, under Hugh O'Neale, 4th Earl of Tyrone, lead the "Flight of the Earls" from the unequal task of defeating the English in the seemingly unending battle for supremacy in Ireland. Hugh, after inflicting many humiliating defeats on the enemy realised he could never win, decided to leave his unhappy country for France and Spain, along with his family and retainers; accompanied by the Earl of Tyrconnel and his family. Many O'Neale's reached Spain, and many prospered by marrying into established aristocratic families with lands and vineyards around Jerez. Timothy, who had married locally, established his Jerez bodega in 1724. Rafael was the last of the O'Neale's and the name disappeared in the 1970's, but such was the fecundity of these old Catholic families, you may be sure many O'Neale's are still in the wine game as well as in the armies of Spain and France as soldiering above all else was their forte.

**OSBORN** Thomas came from Devon at the end of the 18th century, and joined Lonergan & White, bankers and merchants. He was also befriended by the Consul, Sir James Duff. One might say that with that start to his career in Spain he could not fail to succeed, and one would have been right. He came firstly to El Puerto de Santa Maria, and that is where you will still find the company headquarters today. Thomas had been advising Duff Gordon for many years, becoming a partner in 1833. By 1836 he was in sole charge, and ever since the Duff Gordon bodegas have been owned by his descendants. Once again an Anglo expatriate married into a Spanish family, and the present head is the Condé de Osborne. In 1837 Thomas built the beautiful bodega of San José.

The Arabs pioneered distillation and the knowledge would have accompanied the invasion of Spain in 710. Brandy was made in other parts of Spain, but didn't seem to have reached Jerez until the middle of the 19th century, when sherry was enduring a periodic fall in sales.

Domecq put Fundador on the market in 1874, and along with Osborne and Gonzalez Bias became the largest makers of brandy in Europe other than France. It then became more important to Osborne than sherry and remains so. The family also built the huge bullring at El Puerto de Santa Maria, the 3rd largest in Spain, which traditionally attracted the great toreros, especially those currently in the news. But unlike the Domecq's, the Osborne's did not seem to be greatly interested in the "death in the afternoon" business. Yet it is "The Toro de Osborne" for which the family is best known to the public. That 40 foot high black image of a fighting bull in the 50's and 70's was the most famous piece of advertising in Spain. I remember seeing it for the first time as I rounded a sharp bend outside Valladolid in 1956. It was so startling I nearly ran off the road. Later, when I had attended a few corrida de toros and observed the 1000lbs of black bull emerging through the gate, blinking, red-eyed in the strong sunlight; stamping his feet in the sand and visibly very, very angry, I always remembered that 40 foot high silhouette, high on the hill outside Valladolid. Alas, a law of 1994 prohibited the sign of the bull, though they continue to be seen in response to huge public protests. It is always gratifying to see the public triumphant and a stupid law modified if not abandoned.

**SANDEMAN** Sons & Co Ltd has two histories; or at least a history in two parts. The first half in Porto (as the Portuguese call the town of Oporto) from 1814; the second half in Jerez at the sharp end of the sherry trade when Pemartin, a Spanish sherry family of French origin, went into bankruptcy. For 57 years Sandeman had been Pemartin's longstanding London agent and in 1879 was owed £10,000, over a million in today's money. In payment they became the owners of Pemartin's vineyards, bodegas, soleras and most astounding of all the Louis Quatorze-style palace, the building of which, its size and magnificence must have hastened Pemartin's failure.

George Sandeman, of a well to do Scottish family in Perth, borrowed £300 from his father; quite a sum and at the age of 25 went to London and used it to hire a wine cellar. He then started his first and only business, as a merchant importing port and sherry; doing the administration in Birchin Lane, Cornhill, from Tom's Coffee Shop. A frugal start to what was to become a large, worldwide affair; and the year was 1790. It goes without saying he knew nothing about port *or* sherry except drinking it; and nothing about business. Truly "where ignorance is bliss, 'tis folly to be wise" and the old adage was spot-on, for within 2 years he had sold over 150 butts of sherry, about 100,000 bottles. His inexperience was no deterrent from being the first to ship in a vintage port, the 1790, bottled under his own name. In business, beyond doubt timing is of the essence, and by 1792, England and Britain was the wealthiest country in the world and ready to celebrate its leadership in the Industrial Revolution. Great houses were built, art collections were the rage, workshops and factories (or manufactories as they were called) were designing and making the most exquisite furniture and porcelain. Spend, spend, spend said the middle and upper classes, and the French called the British soldiers "rosbif" because they ate masses of meat that Europeans could not afford. Drink was not ignored, and though the French War temporarily prevented Claret and Cognac crossing the Channel it was boom time for sherry and port. War on land or sea hardly interfered with these, and George Sandeman worked round the clock, quartering the country, visiting all the wine buyers. Travelling conditions, roads and lodgings were terrible, but he earned enough by 1794 to buy his own London premises at 24 Old Jewry. By that time George's father had joined the landed gentry, and in Scotland, unlike in England, there was no stigma attached to reaching the top of the heap through trade.

By 1800 George had become the London agent for Sir James Duff, the much loved and revered British Consul at Cadiz; and Duff, a fellow Scot, had been a shipper and exporter since at least 1760. They were friends, the old man and the young thruster. The friendship, though genuine, must have been very useful to George; though in 1805, Duff passed the agency to his kinsman, Sir William Duff Gordon. This was probably a mistake, as Sir William was a bit thick and undoubtedly lazy. I have never had much time for the homily "Blood is thicker than water"; preferring rather "God gives us our relations, we choose our own friends". Nevertheless, Sandeman persevered in Jerez, keeping well clear of all areas of the trade not concerned with buying and selling, to achieve a more than modest success. He made numerous visits to Spain to cement relationships, and to reconnoitre the state of trade; resulting from which he took on the Pemartin London agency, which he held for 57 years. He then took over virtually all Pemartins Spanish assets, and finally established a permanent footing in Jerez. There are no hordes of Sandemans living in Spain or Jerez, like the

Gordons, and no marriages into influential local Spanish families recorded on the family. There was no Sandeman who could call himself a Jerezano.

Despite phylloxera and oidium, the vineyards though seriously affected and requiring much expensive care and attention, gave Sandeman the regular and stable supply of wine for his bodegas. Albert, now head of the family, and the sherry business was appointed Governor of the Bank of England. From that point the family fortunes were secured to the present day, and a Sandeman headed the company through 8 generations. I suppose there was plenty of excitement in the 200 years from 1790 to 1990, but the best story recorded concerns their Bodega Grande, which caught fire in 1912 while full of oloroso sherry. So hot did the wine become that the alcohol distilled. Most of Jerez turned out with pots, pans, buckets or anything that could hold the liquid that flooded the gutters. It was fiesta day, a gift from Heaven, just as in the film "Whisky Galore" when the Scottish Islanders pirated the cases of whisky from the cargo of the shipwrecked on their beach.

**TERRY** Fernando was the descendent of the Terry family that left Ireland in the 17th century to escape religious persecution, and ended-up in Jerez; and like other Irish, prospered in the wine business. Their properties were mainly in El Puerto de Santa Maria and they distilled brandy, as well as making wine.

After the 1865 phylloxera wipe-out, Fernando put Terry's together and created a large and successful family business. He was one of the early growers to appreciate the need of heat exchangers. One of these inserted into the must before the commencement of fermentation, conducted away much of the terrific heat generated by the fermentation process.

Absence of the use of heat exchangers, especially in hot climates, was the main reason for great variation in wine quality, and the destruction of what might otherwise have been a good vintage. Like many successful family businesses Terry was first bought by Harvey and then Allied Domecq.

The family was perhaps even better known for horse breeding, a tribute to its Irish ancestry. Later the beautiful Harmony Bodega became the stables for the Terry horses. A very Irish thing to do.

These expatriates were all born in England, Scotland and Ireland.

Not all were Anglo Saxons but all influenced by the Protestant way of life which developed from when Martin Luther nailed his theses against indulgences to the door of his church in Wittenberg in 1517. Those names could be augmented to 150 or more of those who made their way to the area of Jerez, San Lucar de Barrameda, or El Puerto de Santa Maria between the beginning of the 17th century and the early part of the 20th. Their reasons for going there were many, but if we accept the Celtic Irish and Highland Scots who came because of religious or political reasons, the others came as free men, able to move easily between the United Kingdom and Spain to make their living from sherry in some way. They certainly did not come for an easy life. They were not peasants, but were born into, or had risen into, the middle class, and knew exactly what they were about. The cold, damp winters, sunless summers and full cloudy days were left behind as they moved to the small enclave in Andalusia which was Jerez, and the weather different but better. Hot, almost unbearably hot Summers but mild winters, with primitive living conditions and the constant threats of cholera, typhoid and even plague. A better climate would rarely have been a reason to take up a semi or permanent residence in a foreign, even bizarre, country. They came from places where everyone was protected by Habeas Corpus, trial by jury and Common Law dating from the Norman Conquest, to a country still not free from feudalism, and a religion that was a constant menace to freedom of thought and speech. It may not have been read in the Catholic Bible but the admonition of St Paul on master and man relationship would have been well known:

> *"Let every soul be subject to the higher power*
> *For there is no power but God*
> *And the powers that be are ordained by God"*

Spain, whatever your class, must have been a daunting place to live in for an Englishman, an Irishman or a Scotsman.

They came to enter the sherry business; not as labourers, vinedressers, or as anybody subject to Pauline admonitions. Yet the Jerezanos had been making wine for sherry in a knockabout or even disciplined way since the 14th century or earlier. Foreigners from the North coming to work in Jerez might be compared to a bunch of Brummies going to Detroit in 1920 to teach the Americans how to make cars but there was a difference, expats did not come empty-handed or broke. They knew about sherry, at least from the drinking end. They were not without capital, or they knew where to get it, and they had business acumen, commercial and other skills required to build a successful enterprise. Some were of the professions created or required in the fast burgeoning industries of the Industrial Revolution, which in the 18th century had hardly started in Europe, and in Spain was even further away from the starting blocks. The expats knew about exporting finished goods, importing raw materials, and selling the products of workshops, or breweries or distilleries to the world. And they had a hunger for success gained through hard work and the Protestant work ethic.

So why *did* they come? It would be simpler to say to make money, but that I am sure was not the only reason. In any nation, it is usually the best of its people who take chances; take risks, which end-up in death or injury; people who want to make it on their own. Owing nothing to others; depending on their brains and making their own mistakes, and if they fail they start again. Such, in my view, were the expats, or most of them who went to Jerez. Whatever the reason, I am sure not a single one intended to leave the sherry trade poorer than when they arrived. In sherry they saw a product that was marketable on a scale never envisaged. Or more likely, Spain being as it was, the people in the sherry trade had no wish to expand. The growers and the shippers were probably content with their way of life and saw no reason for change, just for money. However, if these Northerners wanted to sell our wine to the heretical masses North of the Channel, let them get on with it as long as they don't frighten the horses.

In a crude manner the expatriates brought the Northern talents of management and organisation to a place that thought they had talents enough. Not as a prepared plan, but gradually over several generations. They started by buying the best wine, then found the best shippers for moving the wine to London, Dublin, Edinburgh and other towns. They learnt about viticulture and how to identify the best growers and vineyards from which would come the best wine for blending into sherry. They bought into shipping and started to sell their own sherry, under their own name to their own agents in London and elsewhere. They and their agents developed the largest markets of the time, which were the UK, South Africa, Australia, USA and Canada; and to those were added Scandinavia and Northern Europe in general. Despite the vicissitudes of wars, plagues, slumps, inflation, deflation and crop failures, these expats played a leading part in creating a world market for the marvellous sherries of Jerez. And it would not be unfair to say that without their arrival and intervention, the market would never have been developed. They were also good immigrants, the sort that brings great benefit to a country, and in Jerez quickly turned themselves into regular Jerezanos.

# 7

# THE SUPREMACY OF THE MEDOC

"All right, I'll buy the place as long as I don't have to drink the bloody stuff". "The place" was Château Latour, the year was 1962, and the speaker Viscount Cowdray; later owner of the Financial Times. The Pearson Group of newspapers, Cowdray Park, the premier venue of polo, and soldier of the Sussex Yeomanry, who successfully escaped from Dunkirk in 1940, but carelessly left his left arm behind in France. That sentence must have been the most astounding ever recorded in the annals of vineyard sales in the Medoc. Latour was up for sale to the relief of its many shareholders, and was thought a snip at £1,750,000. Cowdray was asked to buy it and he bought a controlling interest for £900,000. Of the remainder, Harveys the sherry merchant's, bought 26%, and the owners of Château Beaumont the rest. Cowdray admitted he preferred Scotch and looked on Latour as a piece of real estate rather than a great wine Château.

Since that first taste of Château Lafite in August 1944, my belief in claret as the greatest red wine that ever grew on planet Earth has never wavered; in fact it continues to strengthen. If good weather alone produces good wine, Bordeaux and Burgundy would hardly ever have been heard of. The professionals, if they hold the same opinion, it tends to be qualified by the torrents of decent reds that flood into the UK from Australia, Italy, New Zealand, South Africa, Chile

# THE MÉDOC

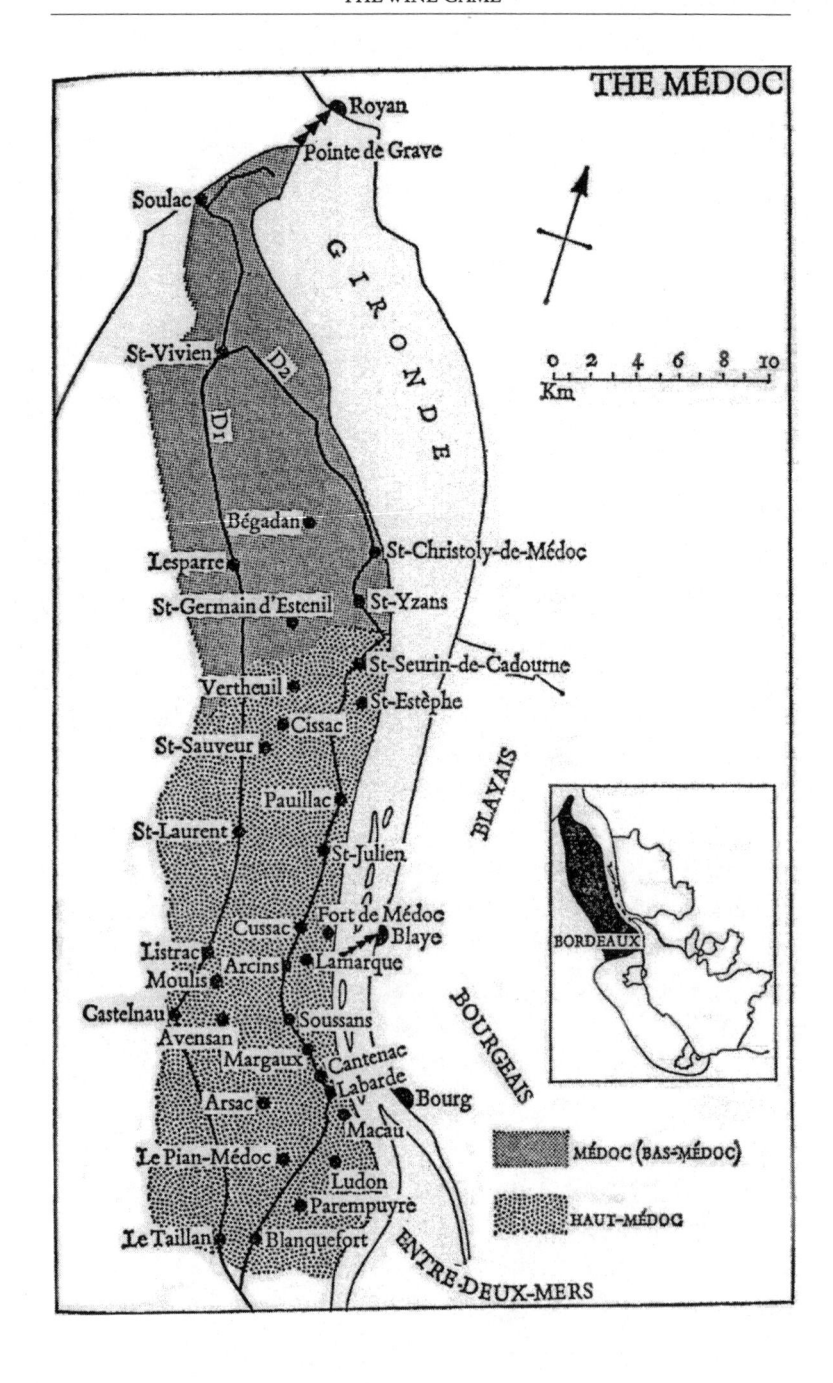

and California, and they would be unwise not to take a strong, independent view; global in fact. The customers demand it. To paraphrase Voltaire, I might not take Voltaire's advice, and defend to the death my opinion that the Grand Crus of Medoc reds are without equal, but I believe it. I believe also that only greed and stupidity will bring them down. They are capable of both.

So why the Medoc?; as usual we must look to our formidable ancestors, the Phocaeons of Greece and the Romans. The Phocaeons founded Marseilles in about 600 BC and planted the vine; which by 600 AD had taken root in all the suitable parts of what we today call France. Whatever weather-changes that might have happened between then and now, the Greeks would have found the shores of southern France not dissimilar from Greece where the vine had flourished for aeons. So, as settlers looking for a new home, they planted and started a wine industry.

They did not penetrate North. The Celts were already over the Alps from Italy, and settled in and around the valley of the River Isère on the East bank of the river Rhône, where the first vineyard in France thought to be Hermitage was planted by the Celts. A certain irony there as Hermitage was one of the strong and excellent reds used about 1800 years later to beef up the puny Medoc reds. Then Caesar's legions, speedily marching North, following and no doubt using the Rhône where navigable, planting the vine wherever, and everywhere that had the good fortune to be conquered by Rome. Both sides of the Rhône estuary were planted in the area later to be called Provence and further West and Midi. As the march North hastened, in an astonishing short time certain regions began to gain reputations. Those of the Rhône Valley, and then the wines of the Garonne and the Gironde, that is to say, the Medoc. For the Romans pushed hard up those rivers which flowed West and North West. Prescience seemed to have played a role when the peoples of the Gironde estuary, the slopes of Burgundy which became the Côte d'Or, and later the Rhine Valley knew that their climate and soil would create the world's greatest wines. Though they could never have known that much further South would grow larger crops in more fertile soil. But perhaps it was not prescience but the absence of roads that isolated the great growing area from the fecund South with its navigable rivers and Mediterranean ports. To be successful in industry whether with wine or cars or anything else, needed roads or water. In the South there were rivers and the sea. The rest of France had virtually no roads, great areas of the country were isolated from each other for hundreds of years.

The military roads constructed by the Romans had all but disappeared from sight by 600 AD and had not been replaced but wine had to be moved and to do it using paths or tracks on crude carts; barrels weighing 200lbs or more; leaking as likely as not, would have been difficult, and it is doubtful if journeys of a few miles took less than several days. So transport methods by water or tracks, best sites for planting by the early settlers was done solely by those in the South under the influence and training of the legions. The commercial skills came from the Italians who had set-up offices and entrepôts around Lyons, for the purpose of gathering wine and transporting it all over the Eastern part of the Empire. The Romans established strict control over the wine business using a pair of mercantile associations. The *Negotiatores vino internates* serving the Eastern Mediterranean, and the Negotiatores vino supernates with territory authority up to the Adriatic ports. Such authority and administration determined what wines would be planted, and where. Adopting for example the Syrah grape to the northern Côtes du Rhône; and the Pinot Noir to the area between Dijon and Beaune who's delicate thin skins and acidity would not be damaged by the torrid southern sun.

The Pinot Noir grape has never done well outside of the Côte d'Or. The Gamay grape from which Beaujolais wine is made was banned in 1395 by Philip the Bold Duke of Burgundy from being planted near to the Pinot Noir in case it should damage the wine by its heavy cropping and coarseness. Inferior grapes in the Beaujolais makes a pleasant enough wine, though nowhere else save in Anjou when blended with Cabernet Franc to make a passable rosé.

Despite the weather in Bordeaux being kinder to the vine and the grape than in Burgundy, it was, and is, far from perfect; and the greatest curse was a bad winter such as 1708/09, which did *so much* damage, the net vintage was a virtual wipe-out. Though this taught the growers a hard lesson. By keeping the small harvest back for inclusion in the crop of next year, the benefit of quality and maturity was phenomenal. Just by allowing that small part of the small crop to blend in the barrel with the new crop had great influence on future practice.

The grower also thought it a good idea to send the wine to the merchants for bottling, as he had never considered bottling important anyway but considered the merchants advice on that matter to be important.

At that time and until well into the 19th century, sales of the Grand Crus Lafite, Latour, Margaux and Haut Brion, was small in France but huge in England, to where it was sent using the admirable sea routes along the Gironde estuary which already had 300 years of experience behind it. Paris knew little of the Bordeaux wines, and it might even have been easier to ship from Bordeaux to Paris via Calais, so bad were the lateral roads East. In fact they hardly existed.

Over the centuries, and largely under English influence, Bordeaux had nurtured an educated bourgeoisie, with a Provincial *Parlement*, not uncommon in France, with a large degree of autonomy. No matter that the Members were mostly lawyers that gave stability and a framework within which to develop trade, particularly the wine trade. And they were usually landowners also, who employed peasants steeped in viticulture, or tenant farmers, as share-croppers, who received from one tenth to one quarter of the harvest. But the peasants usually lacked wine-making skills and their practice after harvest very slapdash, especially in matters of hygiene. The tenants also were not much better. The vineyard owners may not have had the skill either with which to make a sound wine but they knew where to buy skilled help, and they had the money. It was well into the 18th century before the Medoc was producing red wine that would be recognised today as drinkable, and the end of the century before the Medoc wines had attained superiority over all others. Unlike on the Côte de Nuit and Côte de Beaune where the vineyard owners were mostly absent landlords, those in the Medoc had a "hands on" policy and knew how to protect their investment.

The success of the Grand Crus, and of course the best of the lesser growths depended on the skill of the vineyard régisseur; a difficult word to translate but "steward" may do. His tasks are manifold, which vines to plant, and where, (Cabernet Sauvignon, Merlot, Cabernet Franc, Malbec) and in what percentages. Each would be vinified separately and kept in separate barrels. Then came the critical operation of the *assemblage*. This was the responsibility of the régisseur assisted by the Maître de chai, the cellar master.

What percentage of this grape and how much of that. He would of course have decided on which day to start picking, when to declare fermentation was complete, and when to wrack the wine off the skins and stalks. These operations and others form the largest cost of wine making; thought if your market was local and domestic, errors were not important but in building-up a nationwide and international market, the avoidance of error was paramount.

Having spent a lot of money to make a good wine of enviable reputation, the great obstacle remained, getting it to London and other places in prime condition. It was contained in barriques of Limousin oak. A barrique held 225 litres and four of them formed a tonneau, which was just an expression of quality *not* a container.

For many years there was little or no French bottling; neither at the vineyards nor in the merchants' cellars. London received the barriques and did the bottling *en masse*. The wine could be ruined if the bottling and corking was not of the best; and London bottling *was* the best. Why? Because in the 18th and 19th centuries, the UK led the world in engineering and production practices, and bottling plants for the whole of the world were designed, built and exported. London bottling of claret was respected by the Medocain, as something they could not equal; or for that matter wanted to do. It was many years before you could with confidence, read on a bottle "Mis en Bouteille au Château".

The most elegant name in London Bottling was Berry Bros & Rudd wine importers since 1698, for generations they bought the great wines of the Medoc in casks and bottled them in their own bottling plant; and were still doing it in the 1970's. Tony Rudd claimed that the French Châteaux do the bottling when they have a couple of hours to spare, but not necessarily at the right time or on the best equipment.

The reds of Bordeaux had been imported with but few interruptions for over 300 years, but a milestone of note must have been the wine auction set-up by Christie Manson & Woods (Christie's for short) the London Auctioneers in 1776. Though at that time Claret had but modest sales in England, the market having been taken over by Madeira, Sherry and Port. Soon after, the great Clarets, the Grands Crus and Christie's are usually linked as representing quality, price and prestige. You need only consult Michael Broadbent's massive 432 pages of "The Great Vintage Wine Book" to read about harvests, weather and tastings of Grands Crus from 1771 to 1978. An astounding record of continuity. And it is of course from that period of roughly the mid-18th century that England became the principal target of the Medoc Estates. Because England was the wealthiest nation in the world, and its wealthy citizens from an ancient land, rich aristocracy and clever hard working industrialists were ready to buy the best of everything without counting the cost.

Viticulture has always suffered badly from diseases. One of the worst is Oidium, better known as powdery mildew, which can destroy a vintage if not caught early. As far back as 1848 it was first seen in a Margate greenhouse. Oidium came from America and could be controlled by spraying with powdered sulphur, a most unpleasant task. Wine growing was thought as an art, but it took the bio-chemist to save the industry and his many chemical developments which are in general use today, and without which, the industry could not survive, whatever the organic freaks say. But the one which could have destroyed all the French vineyards, and nearly did, was Phylloxera Vastatrix. Aptly enough "vastatrix" means "devastator". This also was accidentally imported from America. An insect from a greenhouse in

Hammersmith was sent to Professor Westwood, a botanist and entomologist at Oxford, and he identified it as Phylloxera, which in due course slowly and surely killed every European vine it came in contact with. It could have wiped out most of the world's wine industry. It is an aphid that feeds on the root and had been so long at home in America on native vines that in time they built up resistance. American vine root stocks had been imported into France because they were cheap, and the devastation caused is now a nightmare of history. It was many years after the first sighting in the mid-1880's that it was eliminated by grafting the European vitisvinifera vine on to the Phylloxera resistant American root stocks. This catastrophe in France was comparable with the potato famine of Ireland in 1848–52, though happily without deaths. Except perhaps more than a few suicides. It was a sad business and hundreds of small vineyard businesses were bankrupted. The best book on the subject in English is "The Great Wine Blight" by George Ordish.

France in the 18th and 19th centuries, despite the Revolution was a low wage economy. The Revolution of course was a middle-class affair, and the middle-classes viewed the proletariat with the same scorn, as did the aristocracy. The workers on the estates, the men and women who pruned and dressed the vines, weeded and hoed between the rows, gathered the harvest and treaded the grapes received one franc a day if you were male and fifty centimes if female. I fancy obesity was no problem in the vineyards. There was however a free issue of a barrique of wine per family per year, which perhaps stemmed the pangs of hunger. The best that could be said was that the job was for life, for a conservative people who abhorred change. Though when the Revolution did reach Bordeaux, with many an aristocratic and bourgeois head tumbling into the basket, the peasantry must have reconsidered its position vis à vis the man/master relationship.

With Napoleon vanquished in 1815 and only the brief Franco Prussian War of 1870, which hardly affected Bordeaux, peace settled over the Medoc until the horrors of the Phylloxera blight. The Medocain survived; just, though it was more than 10 years before normality of a sort returned. Some wine was produced and paradoxically fetched high prices. Two World Wars did not help, heavy casualties among the peasantry and a general shortage of money gave the wine industry a thin time. Low prices even for the Grands Crus, and the general condition of Europe as a whole was bad for Bordeaux, and it was the 1950's before trade truly recovered with very high prices and a fine living for everybody, even the growers; but especially the merchants, and the shippers.

The great panache of the vigneron and his associates in this ancient trade, throws up extraordinary stories. And I am particularly fond of 2 which cap nicely this chapter on the Medoc and the wines of Bordeaux.

The Russian upper classes had a notoriously sweet tooth in the wine department, which drew them like iron filings to a magnet to the famous Sauternes, who's most famous vineyards of Yquem, Filhot and Coutet were all owned by the Marquis de Lur Saluces an ancient and aristocratic land owning family. There were a series of splendid vintages in the 1880's and the Cruse Family, merchants on the Quai des Chartrons bought the complete 1866 harvests of de Lur Saluces vineyards in Sauternes and Barsac. The Cruse Family was the same one involved in the 1974 Bordeaux wine scandal. Since there was no château bottling, Cruse had the lot bottled in their Bordeaux cellars, and shipped most of it to their Moscow agent. One very important client said to be a Grand Duke of the Romanov's, who was known to be a huge drinker of Sauternes insisted that his Yquem before despatch should be decanted into cut glass decanters, corked and engraved with "Château Yquem" and the vintage year. I recall in January 1945 being entertained with three others by the Russian captain of a destroyer in Travemunde harbour near Hamburg on the Baltic Sea. This was before Winston Churchill's "Iron Curtain" speech delivered at Fulton Missouri in 1945. The outside temperature was -15°c and we were met on the deck by this steward bearing large glasses of Green Chartreuse, which we were expected to down in one, and quick. The captain and others then threw the empty glass at the ward room wall, and we were expected to do the same after the first drink followed by several more. I like to think the Grand Duke did the same with his cut glass decanters when empty. Why not? For Byron wrote "The English upper classes like the sound of breaking glasses".

I hope that story is true, but I have no doubt about the second. The English upper classes in the 18th and 19th centuries were as reckless and feckless as any Russian Boyar, and filled the cellars of their country houses and London mansions with the best wines that Bordeaux, the Medoc, the Sauternes and the Burgundy Côtes could offer. A regular attendee at post war auctions was never surprised when Grands Crus from the Medoc of 1920 and 1970 were offered alongside wines of the great vintages of 1893, 1896 and 1900, remnants of cellars once full of them. Now these examples of the 19th century cellars masters art, I use the word advisedly, would after 50 years or more be only as good as the cork allowed them to be, and a good cork had a life of at least 25 years. So it became the practice of the owner of a great Medoc estate such as Lafite, Latour,

Margaux or Haut Brion to offer to send his Mâitre de Chai over to his wealthy English customers to re-cork the wine and extend its life. It was a splendid idea. The wine owner would have enjoyed the prestige attached to such service, the butler over the moon, and the Mâitre de Chai and *his* master pleased with what would have been a nice little earner and kudos to the Châteaux reputation.

While all this was going on in the splendour of some Palladian mansion in Wiltshire or grand house in Mayfair, one might reflect should the time be between September and December, plying his trade in England, on that other splendid fellow from France, Onion Johnny. With his bicycle festooned with strings of the recent Brittany onion crop, he was a regular visitor year after year on the streets of Southern England and sold the finest examples of the genus alliumcepa, and like those great examples of the wines of Lafite, Latour and the others just as overpriced. Alas Onion Johnny has disappeared; greatly missed; but happily not the great wines of the Medoc.

# 8

# THE 1855 CLASSIFICATION OF THE MEDOC

There was a codification for at least 100 years. Something put together locally and accepted by the vineyard owners, that a small group of red wines in the Medoc enclave were different in those ways in which the workers and owners understood set them apart from lesser growths. What established the "cordon sanitaire" between the great and the others was price, and when that is in place further argument loses value. The perception is everything. I remember a Master of Wine saying, and he spoke *sotto voce*, while looking over his shoulder, that he could find no more virtue in a 1st growth than a 5th growth, though the price difference per case was 10 times. We were talking about the 1961 vintage. I was not so much shocked as intrigued by this jewel of information coming as it did from such an authoritative source. This price difference though astounding in the 80's and 90's was still there 100 years earlier, and who do you think was paying these prices throughout the period? Why, the British of course! It was a long time before our American cousins reached our level of lunacy.

My informant was not *absolutely* sober, but what he said was surely *in vino veritas* of the highest order.

Too often the 1855 has been accorded the same sacred importance as the tablets brought down from Mount Sinai by Moses. But where as Moses tablets broke into pieces, the 1855 Classification has proved unbreakable. From the

## THE 1855 CLASSIFICATION OF RED BORDEAUX

### Premiers Crus
| | |
|---|---|
| Lafite | Pauillac |
| Latour | Pauillac |
| Margaux | Margaux |
| Mouton-Rothschild | Pauillac |
| Haut-Brion | Pessac (Graves) |

### Deuxièmes Crus
| | |
|---|---|
| Rausan-Ségla | Margaux |
| Rauzan-Gassies | Margaux |
| Léoville-Las-Cases | St-Julien |
| Léoville-Poyferré | St-Julien |
| Léoville-Barton | St-Julien |
| Durfort-Vivens | Margaux |
| Lascombes | Margaux |
| Gruaud-Larose | St-Julien |
| Branc-Cantenac | Cantenac |
| Pichon-Longueville | Pauillac |
| Pichon-Longueville-Lalande | Pauillac |
| Ducru-Beaucaillou | St-Julien |
| Cos-d'Estournel | St-Estèphe |
| Montrose | St-Estèphe |

### Troisièmes Crus
| | |
|---|---|
| Kirwan | Cantenac |
| Issan | Cantenac |
| Lagrange | St-Julien |
| Langoa | St-Julien |
| Giscours | Labarde |
| Malescot-St-Exupéry | Margaux |
| Cantenac-Brown | Cantenac |
| Palmer | Cantenac |
| La Lagune | Ludon |
| Desmirail | Margaux |
| Calon-Ségur | St-Estèphe |

### Troisièmes Crus (cont.)
| | |
|---|---|
| Ferrière | Margaux |
| Marquis d'Alesme-Becker | Margaux |
| Boyd-Cantenac | Margaux |

### Quatrièmes Crus
| | |
|---|---|
| St-Pierre-Sevaistre | St-Julien |
| St-Pierre-Bontemps | St-Julien |
| Branaire-Ducru | St-Julien |
| Talbot | St-Julien |
| Duhart-Milon | Pauillac |
| Pouget | Cantenac |
| La Tour-Carnet | St-Laurent |
| Lafon-Rochet | St-Estèphe |
| Beychevelle | St-Julien |
| Le Prieuré-Lichine | Cantenac |
| Marquis-de-Terme | Margaux |

### Cinquièmes Crus
| | |
|---|---|
| Pontet-Canet | Pauillac |
| Batailley | Pauillac |
| Haut Batailley | Pauillac |
| Grand-Puy-Lacoste | Pauillac |
| Grand-Puy-Ducasse | Pauillac |
| Lynch-Bages | Pauillac |
| Lynch-Moussas | Pauillac |
| Dauzac | Labarde |
| Mouton-Baronne-Philippe | Pauillac |
| Le Tertre | Arsac |
| Haut-Bages-Libéral | Pauillac |
| Pédesclaux | Pauillac |
| Belgrave | St-Laurent |
| Camensac | St-Laurent |
| Cos-Labory | St-Estèphe |
| Clerc-Milon | Pauillac |
| Croizet-Bages | Pauillac |
| Cantemerle | Macau |

moment it was handed down by the brokers to the Medoc vineyard owners meeting together on the Quai des Chartrons.

The historic occasion which gave it birth was the Exposition Universal in Paris organised by Prince Napoleon, of a comprehensive display of the Gironde wines, arranged by category. He was not satisfied with the list supplied, based as it was on price reached over the previous 100 years. So the chastened members of the Bordeaux Chamber of Commerce handed over the job of providing the list to the Brokers' Federation. *They* then put together a list, which was generally knowledge to the Medoc growers anyway; it was based on price comparisons. Although to be fair to the brokers, a tasting was put on to back-up what they knew already. After all, that had been their sole job for a very long time; and from that point the list became frozen; except that in 1973 Mouton Rothschild was promoted from the 2nd to the 1st growth, deservedly so perhaps, but also startling. Equal at least to the miracle at Cana during the wedding, when water was turned into wine. Though Haut Brion is in Grave just outside Bordeaux, and it was included in the 1st growths by the brokers who had long considered it to be the best of the lot; smuggled in on the old boy basis.

The List consisted of 62 vineyards, broken-down into 5 groups. 4 in the 1st group, 14 in the 2nd, 14 in the 3rd, 11 in the 4th and 18 in the 5th. People often wondered why wines from St Emilion and Pomerol were not included. They were not, because the 1855 was solely for the Medoc; and in any case the brokers of the Quai des Chartrons had probably hardly heard of any wines grown as far away as St Emilion, 20 miles in the 19th century was no small distance, and in the matter of wine the French remain extremely parochial. The wines of St Emilion were classified in 1955, though not

Pomerol, which contains a real joker in the pack. The wine of Château Petrus had been ignored by the British before the Second World War. After which it emerged like a phoenix from the flames in the mid-60's. Originally 16 acres and still only 30, on a clay outcrop and vinified from the Merlot grape rather than the revered Cabernet Sauvignon of the Medoc, it regularly out prices the 1st growth Medocs. For example, as recently as April 2009, Latour 1970, a good year was on offer at £2,861 a case, and Petrus £10,000 a case; and Lafite 1982 was £8,719 a case and Petrus £25,000 a case. Can anyone explain that?

On balance it might have been better for the public, if not the growers, and merchants had the 1855 Classification never existed. It established such a price gap between 1st growers and the rest; and its unfairness removed incentive from the lesser breeds below the salt to improve their wines. For no matter how hard they tried, they could never either gain access to the 1855; or if on it move up the ladder.

Quality plus price put Petrus into its own class of 1. Superior to the great Château of the Medoc, and put there by market forces, which in the long run will always be the best judge.

There are pratfalls in putting too much trust in lists. Frequently they are created by the powerful to gain authority over the weak. The 1855 which came into existence almost by accident has had that effect; and it gave even more power to the brokers, who, all too often in the past had been like Nemesis stalking the vineyards along with the merchants, deciding whose wine would sell and whose would not, or at least at a much lower price. The 1855 remains frozen in time despite attempts over the years to change its composition; and currently there is no change in sight. The question of quality hardly matters. If you are on the list your wine will always command a higher price then that of your neighbour who is not on it. And if your wine is classed as a 3rd growth, the chances of it reaching a higher price than that of your neighbour classed as a 2nd is remote. There has on occasion been a blip, a temporary loss of nerve or memory by a broker perhaps; but the status quo is always returned to.

Any layman who examines the list is expected to do so with respect if not awe. For are you not regarding everything that is best about the Medoc? The best wines, the best masters of the craft, probably beyond discussion, honest as the day is long. You are expected to accept at face value that these 62 wines are always made from those grapes which when blended together create the most splendid cèpage known to man; and they are Cabernet Sauvignon, Merlot, Cabernet Franc, Petit Verdot, and perhaps a touch of Malbec. And that is taking the broad view. But Bordeaux weather can be capricious and from time to time a poor harvest which, due to lack of sun, but a plenitude of rain will provide the wine with as little as 9.5 degrees of alcohol, when what was required was 11 to 11.5. So out of necessity the growers had to call on providers of wine of greater strength, which had been reflected on in other parts of this book. It is said that where-ever possible the wine from Hermitage was added and there is some interesting evidence about that, the Calvets, wine merchants in Tain Hermitage on the Rhône were suppliers. Octave Calvet first came to Bordeaux in 1870 to sell Hermitage wine to Medoc growers; and I doubt it was for their every day drinking. The Calvets were Anglophiles and Jean Calvet would spend some months in Britain each year visiting customers. Nathaniel Johnston, doyen of that famous Chartronnais Family wrote in his diary that the Lafite of 1795, a fine year "when made up with Hermitage was the best liked of any of that year." The term *hermitaging* was common currency among the merchants.

Perhaps it was the regular additional of Hermitage itself, a most excellent wine which produced the magnificent Medocs. And is Hermitage or others used today to give Clarets the 13 to 14 degrees of alcohol which the customers regularly get from Australian, Californian and others, and now demand; at least in Britain. The greatest scandal ever in the wine trade was brought to light in the Law Courts of Bordeaux in 1974, and the crime was the adulteration of Classed Growths with lesser wines, principally cheap reds from the Midi. As was once quoted in another context by that great 18th century statesman Talleyrand "It was not so much a crime as a mistake".

# 9

## LES QUAI DES CHARTRONS

*Polished floors and even more polished conversations*
                Billiard tables and afternoon tea (Somerville: Ross)

Conveniently near to the docks of Bordeaux, the Quai, at least until the end of the 19th century, housed the city's wine merchants and brokers. In earlier times foreign traders were expected to house themselves outside the city walls. In the end it turned out to the merchants' advantage since the Chartrons (which takes its name from a Carthusian Monastery) are virtually alongside the docks, where the merchant would have his wine cellars and offices. The Dutch, as was often the case, were in the 18th century the first foreign wine traders to arrive and as is also frequently the case the Anglo Saxons quickly followed, to dominate the non-growing end of the Bordeaux wine business with arrivals from Ireland, England and Scotland. So that before the 18th century had barely started, the ethos of the Quai des Chartrons was Anglo Saxon Protestant, and that of an exclusive London or Colonial club. Significantly as in other wine growing and exporting areas of Europe, particularly in exporting, such as Jerez in Spain and Oporto in Portugal, the foreigners came, established themselves and took over. They certainly did not come empty-handed and no doubt were able to establish lines of credit with their homeland. So you will find names such as Barton, Johnston, McCarthy, Lynch, Lawton and many others; Irish Catholics, Ulster

Protestants, Anglo Irish Protestants, and any pure English Protestants if there is such a thing. The question of which branch of Christianity you bowed your head to was not without significance in those days but it rarely interfered with business. There were also Huguenots, very important ones too. Protestant refugees from France itself who became merchants on the Quai des Chartrons and joined the British both in trade and marriage.

When the Anglo Saxon raiders (not an inapposite word) infiltrated the centre of the Bordeaux wine trade based on the town of Bordeaux, it was accidental pure and simple. They came from Ulster, mainly Presbyterian Protestants, and from the other 3 provinces of Munster, Leinster and Connaught. Mainly Anglo Irish who worshipped in the Church of Ireland, Church of England (C of E) by another name. There were middle and upper class Irish too, usually on the run from English religious and political persecution. The McCarthys and the Lynches both followed James II into exile after the Battle of the Boyne in 1690 at the hands of William IV. They left for France with the French troops. The Catholic Irish exiles joined the Irish Brigade which regularly recruited from the Old Country for over 250 years, and may have ended-up in Bordeaux when they had had enough soldiering. The wines of the Medoc were better known in Ireland anyway than in England, as they drank more per capita than the English largely because the Anglo Irish Ascendancy, the gentry who were the ruling order were wealthy and inclined to drink heavily of the best wines. It was said that in England even a gentleman on £1000 a year rarely had wine in the house; but in Ireland a gentleman on £100 a year would feel free to drink himself insensible. The Scots also, would buy French wine by the hogshead and sell it in the streets of Edinburgh by the jug-full as soon as the boat unloaded its cargo in nearby Leith, where also it was bottled for sale in the North of England. At that time in the early 1700's bottling of French wine may not even have started in England. Now the English, the future Chartronnais had sound business reasons for taking the sea route to Bordeaux. A good handful in London would have a business for the importation of port wine from Oporto, and Jerez regularly supplied London with sherry. The trade with Bordeaux was a natural extension of wine trade from the Medoc within the loose business framework that already existed, using the small ports along the Gironde estuary. Taking small cargoes of wine for speculative trading. The Dutch were the first foreign merchants in the late 17th century to take root in the Chartrons and established le quartier Hollandaise. But it was the Anglo Irish who set the Anglo Saxon pace in the first quarter of the 18th century; putting up a commercial organisation, expressly to build an export market of the best Medoc wines from the most prestigious estates to supply a waiting British public. The Irish were largely content with lesser but still good wines; and the Scots would drink whatever they could get, provided it was French.

The Irish as usual had their own way of doing things and were not all that fond of the pure untouched Medoc red. Their preference was for a wine that intoxicated quickly and pleasantly. If the French would not send it; well then, they would have it done in Dublin. There was no shortage of alcohol in Ireland, within the law or outside of it to do the doctoring. Whereupon the French, being nothing if not pragmatic, blended the wines of the Medoc with much stronger wines from Spain or the sunnier parts of France, to satisfy the Irish or anybody else for that matter. *S'en faire rien*, and a Gallic shrug and it was done. As Karl Marx said

"From each according to his abilities to each according to his needs." Though I don't think he had French wine in mind.

If such practices were to be done, it was best done by the grower who had the skills not to make a mess of the operation. To some extent the Medocain had been doing it for years and did not like what was illegal to slip out of their control; but once the barriques were shipped and on their way Northwards, control was lost. So the French growers and later the foreign merchants in their cellars on the Quai des Chartrons did the blending in accordance with the requirements of the customers.

One of the sloppy practices of the Medoc vignerons had been to leave the stalks with the grapes during fermentation. Stalks, a great source of tannin left the wine hard and harsh. This, the vignerons knew, but didn't care. But they discovered the addition of powerful reds from the South soften the Medoc wine and made it drinkable sooner. Later the vignerons learned the practice of *égrappage* removing the stalks before fermentation.

There was an old wine book written in 1824 by A L Henderson, and in it he describes something called *travail de l'Anglaise*. This consisted of adding to a hogshead (52 gallons) of Bordeaux

> 3 to 4 gallons of Alicante red or Benecarlo red
> half a gallon of stum wine
> small quantity of Hermitage

So the buyer received between 8–10% of a wine of which he knew nothing. Just about everybody in the Bordeaux wine trade must have known about adulteration, or blending which was the preferred term. Growers, brokers, merchants, shippers, but probably not the buyers. On "a need to know basis" why tell *him!* One wag is credited with saying "A drinker might think he was tasting a 1st growth when it wasn't even a 5th."

While all this frantic Anglo Saxon vinous activity was going on the French Market was not so much quiet as moribund, sunk in lassitude, and Paris did not even seem to have heard of the Medoc and its famous reds until nearly the end of the 18th century. The Bordeaux bourgeois land owners, and vineyard owners, usually the same people, were greatly troubled by the "Anglo Saxon invasion", but what could they do? No laws were being broken, other than what they were breaking themselves; and beyond the slightest doubt they were good for business. The sales of the most expensive wines from the best-known growers were being exported to the UK in ever expanding quantities. The Bordelais might have considered the English "cold, calculating, over disciplined and rich," but they knew on which side their croissant was buttered. So they joined in, learnt, and became rich as well, and for all their tough business practices the Chartronnais were considered as honourable men who kept their word and paid their bills. They built their fine houses on the Quai des Chartrons, along with capacious cellars, and on the Pavé des Chartrons. The cellars were sometimes several hundreds yards long beyond the offices, holding the equivalent of millions of bottles, and where the blending and ageing took place. Work and expense, which the vineyards were happy to pass on.

The vignerons having pruned, harvested, fermented and put the wines into barriques of 225 litres for maturation, thought their work was finished, and people would come and buy the wine. That, in essence, was what the Chartronnais found when they had settled in, but it was not stable business practice capable of creating growth, particularly of export. It is often thought that the famous châteaux (Lafite and the others) are of considerable antiquity. Not so, no wine estates in Bordeaux are the equal in age of the old monastic clos of the Burgundian Côte d'Or. Until the 17th century there were no large estates, and the vineyards were worked by peasants or tenant farmers. The oldest of the great chateau is Haut Brion which is in Grave outside of the Medoc and dates from 1550; Lafite appeared later. The large estates were owned by the old aristocracy, who had no great interest in how their wine reached the table. Through profligacy and poverty they were gradually replaced by lawyers and the *haut bourgeoisie*, who bought up the land cheaply. They were the only people with hard cash; and it was this influential group on whose toes and feelings the Anglo Saxons trod. Though in the course of a generation or so the Anglos married into them; and before long the French became Anglicized, and the Anglos Frenchified but not too much!

Thomas Barton, the grandest of the Barton clan, who arrived in 1712, was rich enough by the mid-century to buy Château le Boscq in St Estephe, and an estate in Tipperary back home for £30,000, a huge sum, did not take too kindly to being called "French Tom" to his face. When Tom arrived the profession of broker had existed for centuries. They had previously been called "courtiers", and because of the high level of crime in the countryside due to grinding poverty, the courtiers, acting as guards would escort visitors round the estates. In Tom's time a broker had the regular job of middleman between the merchant and the grower. He knew both parties, warts and all; he knew the wines, and through years of practice would develop a palate and incomparable memory. As a taster he would be scrupulously honest. Often despised he worked on a commission of from 1% to 1½% of the purchase price, and probably played the ends against the middle to increase his commission. The broker would taste the wine, and with a piece of chalk mark the quality on the barrel; and if the grower dared to rub out the chalk mark, no broker would ever sell that grower's wine. Feared perhaps, hated a little also, through probity the broker earned authority, and was indispensable to both buyer and seller.

The broker in a way could be compared to the jobber on the old London Stock Exchange up to about 1970. The jobber was the sergeant, the stockbroker, the officer, but the jobber had the skill, the knowledge and the wits. The stockbroker often had none of these. However, that comparison could not be made in Bordeaux because the merchants on the Quai des Chartronnais, had the wits, the money and soon enough developed the skills and the knowledge.

It became a cosy arrangement as, armed with the information passed to him by the broker, the merchant could almost dictate the purchase price. On the other hand he took the long view and understood the meaning of *enlightened self-interest,* would make friends with the grower and enter into an agreement, an "abonnement" to buy his crop or a part of it for a period of 5 or 10 years. A merchant's trust in his broker was absolute. He might say to him that he needed, say, 100 casks of a particular wine, confident he would obtain them, even though he might need to buy from several growers to make up the 100. The Lawton Family came from Cork in 1739, they became brokers, the only brokers to be admitted to the closed fraternity of the Chartronnais, and held the role for over 200 years. They kept detailed records of Medoc vintages, weather records and prices paid to brokers over the whole period, and it was that which strengthened the authority of the Chartronnais in

Bordeaux. So, comfortable in his shabby offices, with no visible signs of expensive living habits, a merchant over many years would build-up a data base of information that gave him the power it takes to create a large and successful business trading internationally in wine. Information has always been the source of power and success and it was this tool, one might almost say weapon, the merchant made and then used to build-up his conglomerate of buying wine, blending it, ageing, and shipping it to his agents in various parts of the UK and if he had good luck also, the owner of wealth worthy of Croesus. While he succeeded, others failed, or did less well. This, Adam Smith, 18th century Philosopher and economist would have approved of and understood.

Merchants usually started as buyers, which was usually their only business skill. But much more was required. In advising which wine to buy, the broker became the link; and together they would assess all the characteristics of the wine particularly those that governed maturity, and drinkability. For the quicker it matured, the quicker it could be sold. In the 18th century, the English had no interest in keeping a wine for years before drinking it, and as soon as it came they would start to drink it. The one thing the merchant could do without, was casks of wine hanging about in his cellar. Ideally he would prefer the casks to be delivered directly to the ship. When he had confidence in his judgement, wine would be bought soon after fermentation was finished for delivery to his cellar purpose built for controlling the ageing, and blending as required. He would, in fact, take on all the duties of négociant, éléveur, wholesaler, treatment of his own wines and shipper. Some Chartronnais of course completed the circle by buying vineyards; but you needed to be a canny businessman before doing that.

Little seems to have been known about machine made bottles in Bordeaux until an Irishman in 1723 built a plant on the Chartrons. It was the first in France. By 1789 he and others were making over 3,000,000 a year by a combination of primitive machines and manual operations. At that time few vineyard owners or merchants were interested in bottling and it was many years before they did. There is evidence that Lafite did some bottling in 1846, according to André Simon that formidable Frenchman who wrote so well on food and wine for decades in England. Though from 1885 until 1906 Lafite refused to bottle at the vineyard. This may have been because the merchants thought that Lafite like the others required an alcoholic boost, which was best done away from the vineyard. Clearly the British market demanded stability in strength and only skilful blending with Hermitage wine or others could provide that. Curiously Holland and Germany were happy to buy claret in its un-doctored state of 8 to 10 degrees of alcohol. At least they knew what they were buying!

By 1923 something happened to persuade the 1st Growths to bottle as a policy. Haut Brion and Margaux started in 1923; Mouton Rothschild, which was still only a 2nd Growth in 1924, and Latour in 1925. In the 1960's virtually the whole of the Medoc bottled at the vineyard; and among the Cru Classé, that is, the whole of the 1855 Classification, château bottling became compulsory by 1972. It is hard to believe that until the 1960's the vast majority of French wine, not only in Bordeaux was exported in barrels for bottling principally in London. It also begs the question did blending take place at the vineyards? Because if the British wanted their French wines powerful in body before the 1960's, they still wanted them the same after.

When bottling, and dare I say it, blending which may or

not be taking place, moved from the Quai des Chartrons, London, Bristol and other places permanently to the vineyards, it must have been a watershed in the affairs of the Quai and the Chartronnais. The centres of power and control moved and the relationships between vineyard owners, merchants and brokers changed out of recognition. Perhaps to a more healthy one but once the independent buyers or worse the great drinks conglomerates were able to go direct to the growers, all the rules changed. And if the truth be known the cure might have been worse than the disease, and when the hard men arrived at the vineyards, many growers might have wished they were still dealing with the Chartronnais, who understood the expression "live and let live"; were gentlemen and kept their word. London bottling was famous; better than French, and on grounds of quality, its passing was regretted by the Medoc growers.

Many people will have read that superb book about Irish middleclass life at the end of the 19th century. It was called "Experiences of an Irish R.M." The authors were two Anglo Irish ladies, Somerville and Ross and it was published in 1905. They also published a travel book called "The Vine Country" and visited the Quai des Chartrons, early in the 20th century.

> *"It was only when we reached the Chartrons that we began to realise what the wine country could do when it put its mind to it. The great quays were packed close with barrels as far as the eye could follow. Barrels on whose ends were hieroglyphs that told of aristocratic birth as plainly as the armorial bearings on a carriage. The streets were full of long narrow carts like ladders on wheels, laden with barrels, one behind the other, and about every five minutes as it seemed to us, some big ship moved out from the wharf, filled to the brim with Claret, and*

*slipped down the yellow current to the other climes. The Chartronnais; polished floors and even more polished conversation; billiards tables and afternoon tea."*

The Chartronnais were both anachronistic and futuristic, if that is not an oxymoron. For 250 years a handful of families dominated the Wine Trade in Bordeaux; or at least were a dominating influence, despite competition from other foreigners and of course the French. They were the Anglo Saxons, deciding the future of the greatest of French red wines, those of the Medoc; while living in a style both exclusive, and seemingly aristocratic. Distancing others, self-contained, and with a self-confidence and attitude, wholly English and quasi Victorian; up to and after the Second World War. At least that was how the native French saw them. It was said of some of them, though their families had been in Bordeaux for generations, they even spoke French with an Oxford accent! They were proud but hardly devout Protestants, and were big contributors to religious charities both Protestant and Catholic. Schools, hospitals and orphanages received generous support. Ian Maxwell Campbell, a respected member of the community, talked of "The handful of German and English youngsters who spent short periods in the wine traders university city. These well connected students were destined to return to their countries fervent supporters of the wines of Bordeaux and more particularly of the families they had stayed with". Campbell also said "I have never been able to acquire such intimacy with burgundy as with Claret."

There seemed to be a controlled shabbiness in which the dust of ages seemed to lie undisturbed, and also in their dress. They felt secure, comfortable in their skins. Typically English of a certain class, knowing there was no need to put on a show, or display visible evidence of wealth; everybody knew *who* they were. Hospitality was second nature to them; to visitors as well as business associates, friends and hordes of relatives. Open house, plenty of food, drink and amusement. Rather like the Anglo Irish in Ireland but then many of them *were* Anglo Irish. They were also unlike the French haut bourgeoisie, uptight, formal who rarely entertained even the closest of business associates in their homes. Even though the Chartronnais were frequently well married into local society.

It would be wrong to think the Anglos were in the majority on the Quai des Chartrons, they were not; but it was influence, power and wealth which set them apart; out of proportion to their numbers. There is a pleasant seaside resort a few miles away in which they built Summer villas, called Arcachon; and made it fashionable; it still is today with its almost landlocked lagoon, huge sand dunes and sweet smelling pines. Like the British Civil Service in 19th century India, who moved to the cool hill stations of Poona, Simla and Uttimacoor to escape the pitiless Summer heat, the Chartronnais and their families moved to Arcachon away from the sticky August heat of Bordeaux. There was also the Bordeaux Cricket Club, the stables, the steeplechase season, the flat racing season and the Lawn Tennis Club in which the First French Lawn Tennis Championships were held in 1909. This was a Little England in Bordeaux, built-up over generations, where it survived the French Revolution, the 1870 Franco-Prussian War, two World Wars, which did not make them French, but the dual nationality came in handy. The children were mostly educated in Bordeaux, though some went back to UK schools but they remained oddly remote and separate while continuing as an indelible part of Anglo French society.

Good things can't go on forever and the wiser ones on the Quai des Chartron must have known that. For over 700 years the finest wines of the Medoc had been bought by the British. No other country approached such a level of purchase. For over 200 years the Chartonnais had ruled the roost, top of the pile, monarch of all they surveyed. Chose your own metaphor, until the 1960's. The Yanks were coming like a thundering herd, buying the best, and in quantities, settling the prices as was inevitable, to outbid the British. But worse was to come.

On the 18th December 1974, eighteen men were tried and eight found guilty of adulterating and falsely labelling at least three million bottles of fine Medoc wine. Only one went to prison, but the principal felons were members of the aristocratic Cruse family. Those of supernatural hearing might have heard the mournful tolling of a single bell as the Court pronounced sentence. As at St Bride's Church outside Newgate Gaol in the 18th century, which preceded a hanging. Hermann Cruse, who was not involved, committed suicide in shame; he jumped from a bridge into the Gironde River. The Cruse family had intermarried with the Chartronnais community, most of whom had had no knowledge of the great scam that had taken place on their doorstep; but they also would have felt the shame. It was a closed community in which, like Boston, 19th century society, "The Lowells spoke only to Cabots and the Cabots spoke only to God."

1974 was a seminal year in Bordeaux. Nothing was ever the same thereafter and how is it today in the year 2010? Change had to come in any case; it just came quicker. The influence of the Quai des Chartrons had diminished, but the négociants offices remain; still shabby, dimly lit hallways and unsafe staircases. There have been developments on the other side of the river, but only single storey buildings, which don't block the view from the old Quai. Recognising the need to give confidence to international clients, many merchants now store their wine in ultra modern, temperature and humidity controlled warehouses on the city's outskirts; with offices more in keeping with the 21st century. But many of the more ancient families of the Chartronnais have stubbornly remained where they have always been. Ready to entertain with royal abandon either in house or in the many splendid restaurants nearby. The business relationships between the growers, the wealthy chateaux owners, the brokers and the merchants have changed with the changing circumstance, but on a personal basis remain warm. After all, they are related.

Sic transit Gloria mundi.

# 10

# THE SHOT CALLERS OF THE CHARTRONNAIS

Those of whom I have written are but a few of the best known among the close-knit community of the Chartronnais. To me they seemed to be the most interesting of a fascinating group of Anglo Saxons who depended very much on each other. They were outnumbered by the purely English members such as Atkinsons, Raldwins, Fennwicks, Chalmers Alberts, Bonfields, Keystons, Eddys, Wests and Gilbeys. Then, of course, there was the Dutch, German, Swiss and French who together outnumbered the Anglo Saxons. Yet it was the latter who set the pace and the ground rules that ultimately created the world market for the Medoc wines which by general acclaim are the *non pareil* of wines in the world.

**BARROW NICHOLAS** was not a grower, a merchant or a broker, and probably not over popular with the Chartronnais. For he brought a measure of lateral thinking to the Medoc wine game. There had always been some bottling taking place though usually only among the 1st Growths, as far back as the early 18th century when only hand-made bottles were done in small numbers. Your average vigneron usually reckoned his work was done when the wine was in its barrels ready for drinking, or taken away by the merchant. A flurry of interest grew when an Irishman, Pierre Mitchell, built the first glassworks in Bordeaux to make wine bottles in 1723. Pierre was several generations ahead of the game as it was the end of the century before machine-made bottles were readily available, and the three million made a year was but a fraction if the wine makers were to accept bottling, were the trade ready to bottle its own wine. Only in the 1920's did several of the great vineyards start to bottle, and not in a very efficient or hygienic way. And it was 1970 before it was mandatory for châteaux to bottle their own wine.

Barrow was a young Englishman trained at the Montpelier School of Viticulture who, in the 1960's, bought a small property Châteaux Courant near to Margaux. He had teamed-up with an American looking for a project on which to use taxable profits made elsewhere. Before that he had spotted a gap in the bottling market and had designed and built a mobile bottling plant which he hired out to vineyards for them to do their own bottling. The idea was brilliant for no small vineyard could find the capital to install their own bottling plant which would only be used for 2 to 3 weeks a year. There was a great demand for his services as it would allow them to put the price increasing words on the bottle label "Mise en boutaille au châteaux".

With the American Investors he developed the run-down Châteaux Malescosse, which was going cheap and had enormous cellars. Using his wine knowledge and by minutely studying local vintage maps he bought packets of good terroir and planted it. Meanwhile his Châteaux Courant was producing about 40,000 bottles a year. This was a good time to invest in the Medoc. There was a lot of money about from men who had made fortunes in the war, and were looking for a good home for their money. Where better than the Medoc and bottle your own wine on a mobile plant.

What is worse, to be too early with an idea or too late?

Probably the former, but Barrow's timing was impeccable. Within 5 years the mandatory law of châteaux bottling was in place and his mobile plant was available for hire everywhere in Bordeaux. But of course to have winners you must also have losers and Barrow, with his mobile unit for hire, and the vineyards forced by law to do their own bottling must have hurt both the Chartronnais who did a lot of bottling and London bottlers also.

**BARTON FAMILY.** French Tom, as he was called behind his back, left Tipperary in about 1685 where he was born into an Anglo Irish family. Probably a younger son, for he left for France in 1712, working as a factor in Marseilles and Montpellier before settling in Bordeaux in 1715. He seemed to have been involved in various trades as he made a fortune in a few years. He bought an estate back in Tipperary for the immense sum of £30,000 and his riches endowed his family of 6 sons; one became an MP, two became generals, and two lived on their spacious estates. Of the three daughters, two married English aristocrats. In no time at all the Barton's became wealthy landed gentry, entirely due to Tom Barton who created a dynasty that was to flourish in the vineyards of the Medoc and on the Quai des Chartrons. Whatever Tom's fortune was based on it certainly was not wine. Though he did buy Château le Bosq in St Esteph in 1747. By 1725 he formed the most prominent merchant house in Bordeaux, Barton and Guestier. The Guestiers were Protestant Huguenots from Brittany who had escaped religious persecution after the Revocation of the Treaty of Nantes in 1685 by fleeing to Bordeaux.

In the 18th century, Tom was the largest buyer of 1st growths and frequently bought the complete Lafite harvest. His son William joined his father in 1743. The link with

Ireland was never broken and it was William's 4th son who carried on the name in partnership with Daniel Guestier. Hugh Barton was imprisoned during the Revolution in 1794 but escaped and it is said burnt down the local guillotine en route to Ireland where he stayed for some years, but rejoined the company later. *His* son Nathaniel and Daniel Guestier's son were both made partners, and Nathaniel's son, Bertram Hugh, born 1865, the father of Ronald who was until 1969 head of Barton and Guestier. He was followed by Anthony Barton. Ronald lived on at Château Langua Barton and was a very serious grower. He was one of the first to bottle his own wine and very successfully. Even though English bottling, especially that done by Berry Brothers and Rudd, very professionally, was widely admired in the Medoc, and throughout the world.

Hugh Barton bought a large part of Château Leoville in 1821, and later the rest of it along with Châteaux Langua. The two vineyards are joined together but Ronald always said though the soil is the same, and the grapes also the Langua which is a 3rd growth, never makes a wine as good a Leoville which is a 2nd growth.

**JOHNSTON FAMILY.** William Johnston came to France in 1715 as an adolescent to learn the language. The family was Scottish and took advantage of James I to settle in Ulster on cheap land as part of the Ulster Plantation. William stayed for a few years then returned to Ulster; married and was back in France in 1729 to work with Pierre Germe who was a general trader, but set-up on his own in 1734, buying and selling wine. The firm became William & Nathaniel Johnston in 1765 trading solely in wine business. Fearing taxes, the Firm moved briefly to Guernsey, then back to Bordeaux. They had good connections in America. Not surprising as 250,000 Scotch Irish fed-up with the English sailed from Ulster in the 18th century to form the backbone of the new republic. First as soldiers against the English in the War of Independence, then as politicians of whom more than a few became President. In 1807 a family member with introductions from Lafayette went to America and within 2 years had over 1000 customers there. They prospered famously in Bordeaux, and added to their trading interests the purchase of Châteaux Ducro Beaucaillou and Dauzac in 1865; both of which were in the 1855 Classification. Sensibly the family took French citizenship, which consolidated their position on the Quai des Chartron and in local society.

Sometime before the 1st World War, the family which still owned Ducro Beaucaillou started to make sparkling wine by the Methode Champagnoise. This really was breaking new ground; it was a visionary action bearing in mind how today sparkling wine dominates the English market coming from many countries. It is not unusual when a piece of lowlife comes out of prison having been locked-up for grievous bodily harm to be given a party by his family and friends, all getting drunk on champagne!

In 1793 at the height of the Revolution, Nathaniel was arrested with Pierre François Guestier. Neither lost their heads. Hugh Barton was arrested at the same time. Hugh had married Anna, Nathaniel's sister in one of the earliest of the dynastic marriages, which was to give such strength and cohesion to the Chartronnais. The name Nat was usually given to the first-born in each Johnston generation. Nathaniel I, II and III all made their mark on the family business. Nathaniel II sought leases in Tain Hermitage to secure his stock of blending wine. There is strong evidence that blending with brought-in wines was general and accepted as normal among the growers, and merchants both in Bordeaux and the UK. There is evidence also that not only lesser châteaux received blending wines, but the great châteaux also. This history of blending, whether to strengthen, or to stretch a small harvest may be the reason why the middle-priced Bordeaux reds are losing ground to those of Australia, California and Chile to name but three.

The Johnston's prestige was added to when they established cricket as a regular Summer game in the grounds of their magnificent Italianate mansion. The great years were in the 19th century, when Maison Johnston expanded almost exponentially. By 1804 the cellar extended to over 15,000 square metres, and could hold 25,000 barrels plus 2,000,000 bottles. The latter suggests they were already bottling much of their own wine, which at the time was still rare in Bordeaux. They also become part owners of Châteaux Latour. There was even greater expansion during the Second Empire of Napoleon III from 1852–70; and in 1876 just before phyloxera struck, exports topped a million pounds sterling. It took several generations of Johnstons before complete recovery was reached after the destruction caused by the phyloxera; not until 1950 in fact; and Nathaniel Johnston Fils under the management of Denis, Archibald and Invanhoe now carry on the great tradition of the Chartronnais 250 years after the company's foundation by the young Ulster Irishman William Johnston.

**LAWTON FAMILY**. The two principal brokers in the last 200 years in Bordeaux were the Franco Dutch firm of Baguenard & Merman, and the Lawtons, who are still trading and the only broker to have been accepted by the Chartronnais as "one of us". Today Hughes Lawton SA is managed by Hughes' son Pierre, the 8th generation of brokers, and the Lawtons have been selling the great growths of the Medoc (Lafite, Latour et al) since 1739. Baguenard was the only broker used by the English merchant Walter and Alfred Gilbey when they were major claret buyers in the latter quarter of the 19th century, and Baguenard was succeeded by the Lawtons. The Mermans were Dutch Protestants so they also would have fitted comfortably into the commercial ethics and ethos of the Anglo Saxon Protestants.

Abraham Lawton, a Cork man, arrived in 1739. His first interest was in shipping and general trade. I never understood what is meant when a person is said to be "in shipping" but suspect it means that when a producer needs a ship somebody "in shipping" knows a friend who has a boat with available capacity.

Within a year of arriving from Cork, Abraham had formed a broking company with Taster, a Frenchman, taking into partnership as Taster and Lawton. From that date 1740 the Lawtons are the only brokers to have survived. That Abraham should have come from Cork is interesting. As early as the 16th century, wines and spirits were smuggled from Irish ports into England to evade excise duty. Henry VII ended that by making Cork and Kinsale and 14 other Irish ports as "wine ports", where presumably incoming wines had to pay duty. So Abraham must have known the "ins and outs" of the Irish/Bordeaux wine trade extremely well when he arrived in France. In fact it is probable that when he went to Bordeaux he had a good idea of the nature of his future, and within a year his first shipment to Ireland was to the Firm of Hugh Lawton. Hugh became Mayor of Cork in 1776. So when the Lawtons were settled in Bordeaux, Ireland became a good customer. The Family forged the link stronger by taking French citizenship just before the

Revolution. That is why Abraham's son William became one of the most powerful figures in Bordeaux during the Napoleonic period. "All powerful" as members of the Chartronnais acknowledged. The Lawtons were Anglo Irish, well to do members of the Ascendancy who ruled Ireland as vice consuls from 1640 up to 1922. It was this on occasions hardly concealed show of superiority that irritated the Bordeaux growers and made them suspicious and even in fear of the unholy alliance between broker and merchant, who the growers believed fixed wine prices not entirely to their advantage. Whether that view held water or not, the grower had to accept it was *les Anglais* who gave stability, discipline and confidence to Medoc viticulture; and provided good markets for their wines. Conditions that did not exist before the English and the Anglo Irish set-up shop on the Quai des Chartrons. If there was one thing that terrified growers it was the possession of large stocks of unsold wine. For that reason if for no other they were grateful to the merchant who was prepared to hold stocks for a long time. Both sides were in the game of "pass the parcel". The broker of course held nothing, which was why both sides eyed him with great suspicion while acknowledging he was needed. But his judgement of a wine and skill in knowing its value was priceless. For the greatest scare of all was high prices followed by serious losses. For example, this condition could result if a harvest, which the broker thought would mature quickly and be ready for drinking quickly, failed to do so.

Another curious fact about these quite dissimilar people, the French, the English, the Catholic and the Protestant, was the ease with which they contracted marriage. The Lawtons, the Bartons, the Johnstons, the Guestiers, the Cruses, the de Luzes.

The Lawtons as a family never took their eye off the ball.

They came as brokers and remained as brokers, except for minor forays into merchanting and shipping, post Second World War. Though now they ship great growths worldwide. They have many claims to success in the Medoc, and were clever in anticipating trouble. In June 1973 Hughes Lawton was in the USA with Henri Martin, President of Bordeaux's leading trade association, unusual for a Medocain, a peasant grower who had built up a splendid reputation with his Châteaux Gloria wine, and 50 years of toil and strife. The object was to persuade the Americans to buy more despite spiralling prices. Martin was sure the Americans would pay, Lawton was sure they would not, and he was much closer than Martin to the customer. The Americans held out and in a few months the Bordeaux wine scandal enveloped everybody in the Medoc. But there is one prize the Lawtons hold. Daniel Lawton, in the 1970's, broke the spitting record; six feet nine inches across the room into the bucket at a tasting!

**LYNCH FAMILY.** The name is very old in Ireland; Lynches abound all over. Through the centuries it settled down as "Lynch". Though in France where that spelling does not come easily to the Gallic tongue they settled on calling it "Lench" the "en" being pronounced as in "bien". They still of course in the wine business spell in "Lynch".

The Family certainly took part in the Anglo-Norman invasion of Ireland by barons of Henry II led by Strongbow, Earl of Pembroke. So de Lench was a Norman Knight who settled in County Meath and Galway; where between 1484 and 1654 no fewer than 84 Mayors of Galway were Lynches. With England turning Protestant at the Reformation some of them must have paid at least lip service to the heretical new religion, if only to keep their lands and property. James

Lynch, the Mayor in 1493 is said to have hanged his own son for murder when no-one else was prepared to do it. That sounds like a piece of Irish gallows humour of which the Emerald Isle has never been short. In due course, when the Family was settled in France, they followed the practice of Galway and provided several Mayors of Bordeaux. The first Irish Catholics to settle in Bordeaux were the Dillans, McCarthys, O'Bynes and O'Quinns. Later came John Lynch who fought with the deposed James II, defeated by William III at the Battle of the Boyne in 1690. Lynch, with hundreds of other Catholics, returned to France with the French element of James' army. He ended-up in Bordeaux and married a local girl. He prospered though not at first in wine. His grandons, Jean Baptiste and Thomas Michel, were even richer but there is no evidence from whence came the wealth. They own several wine châteaux in the Medoc including Dauzac and La Maquiline in Machau. Jean Baptiste, a devout Loyalist, fled to London early in the Revolution, but returned later, becoming Mayor of Bordeaux in 1809. Having staunchly supported Napoleon, he welcomed General Beresford when he led his British troops out of Spain to enter Bordeaux on 12th March 1814. Jean Baptiste was smart enough to play for both sides when it suited him. How other could he have been Mayor from 1809 to 1814.

The Lynch Family now owned 3 wines of high quality and high value, Dauzac, Moussas and Bages; all three being in the 1855 Classification. Lynch Bages is generally considered to be worthy of inclusion at least in the 4th or 5th Growth and is sometimes called the poor man's Mouton Rothschild, though there is nothing poor about the price!

The Lynch Family were never brokers, merchants, nor shippers and there is no evidence that they were ever members of the Chartronnais, which begs many questions.

They were rich, land owning, makers of Medoc wines of an undeniable high order, and distinctly upper class. But they were Catholics of the old English Norman Irish variety, who had fought the English; and when they could no longer fight them in Ireland they fought them in Europe; members of the Irish Brigade in the French Army. As Irishmen their memories were long and the massacres in the 16th century, Elizabethan wars and by Cromwell in the 17th would not have been forgotten, nor the devastation they left in Ireland. As Tacitus said of his fellow Romans "They created a desert and called it peace".

I have often wondered if they ever properly fitted into the cosy English atmosphere of the Chartronnais.

# 11

# THE MEDIEVAL ROADS OF FRANCE

It might seem odd to talk about roads in a book about wine. Or rather the absence of roads! Well, not really, because roads determine whether an industry remains local; a cottage industry or national. France had few roads worthy of the name until Napoleon's time. It is impossible to believe England was ever so primitive as was France until well into the 19th century. Can you believe this? An official report on the Nievre district in 1844 described the strange mutation of the Burgundian day labourer once the harvest was in and the vine stocks had been burned.

After making the necessary repairs to their tools, these vigorous men will now spend their days in bed, packing their bodies tightly together in order to stay warm and to eat less food. They weaken themselves deliberately.

And according to the diary of Jules Renard in 1889 "In Winter they pass their lives asleep corked-up like snails". And this Winter practice of semi-hibernation had been going on in the country communities of France for hundreds of years.

History was quite clear on this, there had been no serious road building in France, a country of over 200,000 square miles since Roman times. Except that is in Paris, where there were a few roads built running radially. The Roman roads had disappeared; out of sight. When Henri IV travelled outside Paris in the 17th century and until early 18th century he took a team of road builders with him, without which speed of travel would have been down to about a mile an hour. Virtually no road building was started until 1738 and then only roads out of Paris in the direction of the borders. To get from say Bordeaux to Lyons in mid-18th century it might have been best to get to Paris then South a distance of 600 miles and on tracks rather than roads. To travel by foot was faster overall than by horse. Tracks sometimes disappeared into thick forests and didn't come out on the other side. And there were no maps, or at least any that could be relied on!

The dreaded corvée instituted in 1738 was the main building scheme before the Revolution. In some parts, the entire male population between twelve and seventy (not many of the latter) were forced to do 40 days a year on unpaid road building. If a gang was a man short he had to be replaced by two women. Moreover the local people would never use the road anyway. In 1777 in the areas of Rouen, 37,000 unpaid workers and 22,000 horses each worked for 7 days and built only 20 miles of road. It was not until the 1830's that the Government used the methods devised by the Scottish Engineer John McAdam, from which point road building was properly organised. Take a moment to reflect on the time it must have taken before a Medoc vigneron received his blending wine from Southern Spain or Hermitage, South of Lyons.

There was great improvement when *le Grand Projet* of the Canal du Midi, the oldest functioning canal in Europe was dug. It runs for 150 miles from Sète on the Mediterranean through 63 locks and under 130 bridges via Beziers and Carcassone to Toulouse. That would have greatly shortened wine transportation time, as wine from Alicante could have gone by sea to Sète and trans-ship to the Canal. But the leg from Toulouse to Bordeaux would have been on 200 miles of tracks. Also wine from Hermitage could have used the River Rhône to Marseilles and then sea to Sète. This is supposition on my part, but surely the Canal du Midi must have been used to advantage. What a terrible problem and cost to provide a wine much stronger than Claret un-doctored, just to suit the British palate. Canals continued to be more used than tracks, and work began in 1839 on the Canal Latéral à la Garonne. It was finally called the Canal des Deux Mers, the name given to the entire length from Sète to Bordeaux. While this Canal was being constructed so also was the Bordeaux to Sète railway which opened for business in 1857, more or less as the Canal was finished. The railway company then acquired the lease on the Garonne Canal and virtually put it out of business by charging extortionate fees. Railway or Canal, the wine still had to get from Spain and Tain Hermitage to Bordeaux. Modern capitalism had arrived in France, and it took away with one hand what it gave with the other.

## 12

# PORTUGAL: A FEW REMINDERS

In 1942, the Italian-born Cristoforo Columbo in the employ of Ferdinand and Isabella of Spain, set-sail West in the Santa Maria without much idea of where he was heading, although he hoped it was the East Indies. The Pope in Rome had an idea. He got out his mappa mundi, which was rather odd (since in the late 15th century the church still thought the Earth was flat) and drew a line on it from North to South. He then published a Papal Bull declaring that Spain in the name of the church should govern all parts of the World to the West of the line and Portugal all parts to the East of the line. Beautifully simple one might say; decently done and dusted. Of course there were millions of heretics and others, prepared to argue the point vigorously on grounds other than religion. Whether that story is apocryphal, or even untrue; it is true that the Spanish with a Bible in one hand, a sword in the other and the armies complete with commissars of the church created quite an Empire in the West; and the Portuguese did the same in the East.

Now, the only thing most people know about Portugal is that they make and export Port wine. What they don't know is that a small coterie of Anglo Saxon and Scottish people, based in Vila Nova da Gaia, which is on the other bank of the River Douro from the town of Oporto, took a very ordinary, and sometimes quite nasty red wine grown in the upper reaches of the river, and turned it into a luscious,

# PORTUGAL

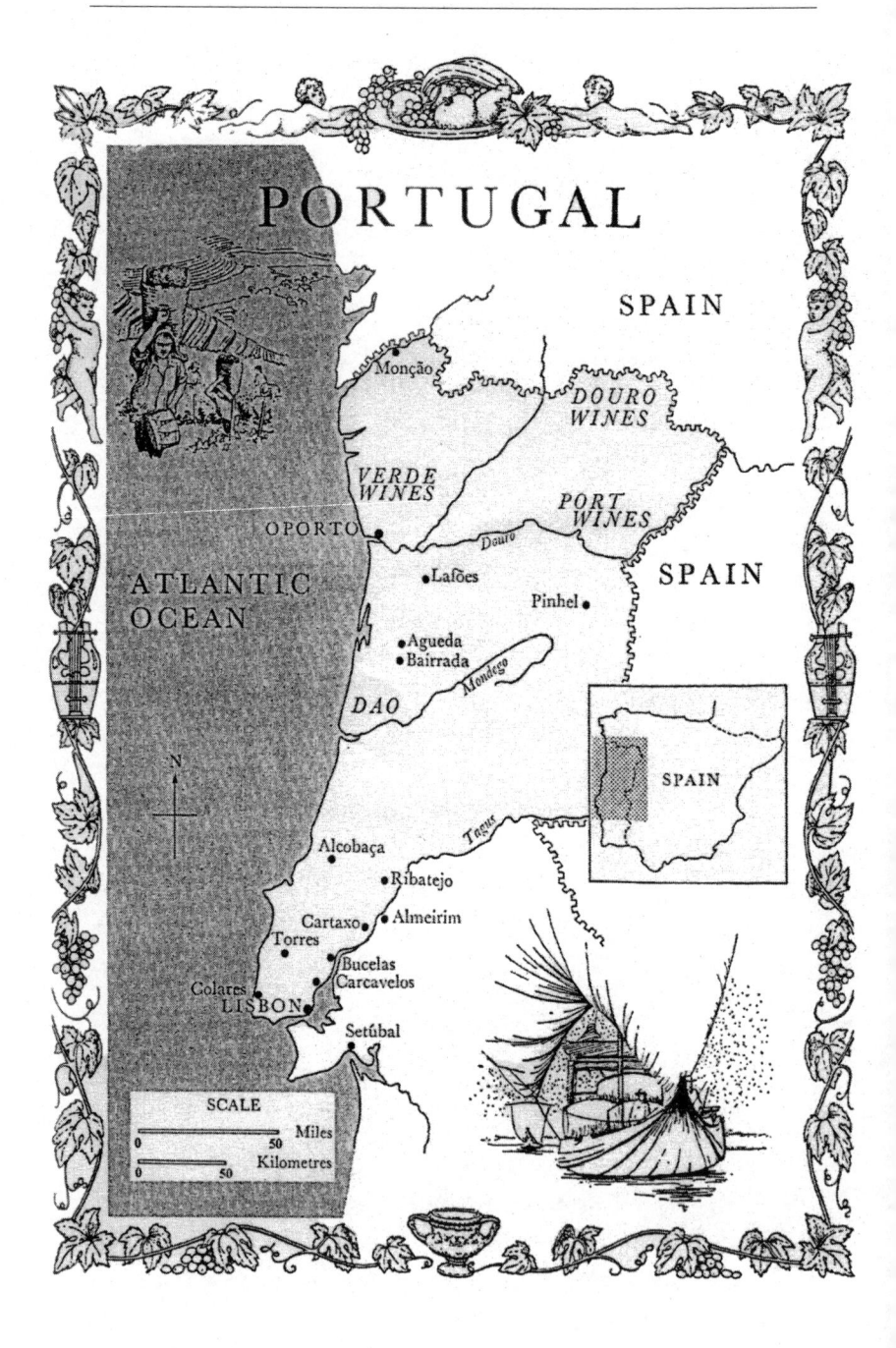

sweet and very comforting liquid called Port wine. They then built-up an industry of blending and ageing and an organisation to sell it ultimately throughout much of the world.

Portugal did not start to pull itself out of the 19th century, until the death of its scholarly but ruthless dictator of 36 years, Doctor Salazar. One of the poorest countries of Europe yet it had a long and illustrious history, and an Empire created by mercantile trading and force of arms stretching from Madeira to Angola and Mozambique; much of the coast in South West India; and Macao in South China. Brazil also became Portuguese but its peasantry and working classes remained in poverty until after Salazar's death. However, with a population of only 11% of the UK and an area of only 35%, unlike us they don't feel as though they are living like rats in a sack. As in Spain, the Catholic Church had held the people in a puritanical thrall; so that the Reformation of the 16th century and the Industrial Revolution of the 18th and 19th centuries, which so enlivened and energised the peoples of Northern Europe, passed Portugal by. It took the death of Salazar to allow democracy to flower and with no bloodshed even though the Communist Party very nearly took over; their failure was due mostly to ridicule. A joke was going around sophisticated Lisbon, which went something like this

> *A Communist activist speaking to a peasant.*
> *"If you had two cars wouldn't you give one to a neighbour?"*
> *"Yes" said the peasant.*
> *"And if you had two cows wouldn't you give one to a neighbour?"*
> *"No" said the peasant. "Why not" said the activist.*
> *"Because I've got two cows" said the peasant.*

Portugal had been an important trading nation since at least the time of that great sailor Prince Henry the Navigator in the 15th century. Lisbon, ideally situated for sailing the oceans in all directions, imported many goods for re-export to the rest of Europe but the land remained undeveloped, agriculture was crude, the people lived primitively, and education and the sciences remained untaught or untouched until well into the 19th and some say 20th century. Wine was the most important export. From time to time when England was at war with the French or Spanish, Portugal's wine benefited from the high taxes exacted on French and Spanish goods. In the 18th century especially, Port wine and Madeira outsold Claret and sherry. It was a 2-way trade; England sold wool or Finished cloth for Newfoundland cod and wine. The Portuguese were the most intrepid Fishermen, and dried codfish was a valuable delicacy, but it beggars belief that a country with such a large, if fragmented wine industry, needed to bring in coopers from England to teach the making of wine barrels. I suppose it was worth it. Though when the British workers were not teaching they were drinking – heavily. Nothing changes.

Thin, white wines were grown North of Oporto. Acidic and low in alcohol, they were not to the English taste. What *they* wanted, and what they got was Port wine, from the middle reaches of the Douro where long and scorching summers produced powerful reds. When a few gallons of brandy were added to each barrel, this was just what the English required but it was only a modest 2 to 3% of alcohol, pushing the table Port wine up to about 14%, and was called Blackstrap. The real Port wine, King of all dessert wines was yet to be made. Blackstrap might not have suited your great grandfather who never drank anything less than a 5th growth Claret; but it was welcomed by the weary masses striving to get drunk. Samuel Pepys knew Blackstrap well. By the late 18th century English workers were fond of very strong sweet tea; it was comforting. But even better was strong alcoholic Blackstrap, which got him legless. Oporto was well positioned to ship its strong reds to Bordeaux whose vignerons used them to beef-up their Clarets for the English, not forgetting the Irish and the Scots. Apart from the Douro reds, there were by the easygoing viticultural practices of the times, better-balanced and quite strong reds from Colares, almost a suburb of Lisbon, and from Dao, South of Oporto. Those I have tasted these last 50 years I would rate better than the bulk of the middle ranking reds of France. Colares is unique, it is one of the few vine-growing areas in Europe that escaped the Phylloxera. After Phylloxera was dealt with, the Portuguese growers did a most stupid thing. Many imported the American Labrusca vines, immune to Phylloxera, but also immune to making good wine. Huge crops, disease-free but robust. It is no accident that Americans call wine made from this grape "foxy". The Portuguese workers got used to its horrible taste, naming it "vinho americano" and still drink it today.

# 13

# PORT WINE? ANYBODY CAN MAKE IT

It may be facetious to say that it is as easy to make Port wine as gunpowder. When I was a fourteen-year-old boy we would steal small quantities of potash, sulphur and charcoal from the school lab to make small bombs (or fireworks as it would be done just before November 5th). The items would be ground-up separately then mixed in a rough ratio of 2-2-1, wrapped in a screw of paper about the size of a toffee wrapper. You then put it on the ground and hit it with a hammer. Depending on whether or not you got the mix right, you got a modest bang or an explosion that rendered you deaf for a couple of days.

To make Port wine you ferment black grapes to a must, which you run-off into another vessel off the skins and, using your experienced peasant's eye, you tipped in brandy or its equivalent to give 20 to 25 degrees of alcohol. Let it settle for a week or two then sell it. Depending on when the brandy killed the fermentation to retain grape sugar, you got a drink which, if you drank it like a table wine, would make your throat raw and half blow your head off! The comparison with gunpowder is, I agree, absurd; but to say "reductio ad absurdum" is permissible.

Port wine, what is it? Well to start with it is as factory made as Champagne or Madeira. You grow red wine then turn it into Port; and not necessarily in the place of growth, which may be as poor agriculturally as where Claret,

Burgundy or Riesling are grown, ground, which wouldn't grow a decent row of carrots or cabbages. The soil is called "schist", which is like slate and must be broken-down with crowbar and pickaxe and much hard labour before the vines can be planted. Then the ground is terraced to prevent the soil, as we can now call it, being washed away by the torrential Winter rains. There is no easy way to get grapes to grow in the Douro.

As was often the case, the hard Protestant men, along with a few Calvinists from North of the Channel arrived late, but finally took over the show. Nobody doubts that Port wine is a British invention; and the inventors decided to make their homes in Portugal.

Parallels can be drawn with Jerez in Spain and Bordeaux in France of course. They were not the first to arrive in Oporto. Christiano Kopke, a German, began trading there in 1638; and by 1650 there were also French, Dutch, Spanish and Italian; all of whom set-up associations to protect their interests; which certainly included shipping wine from the many growing areas North of both Lisbon and Oporto.

The first British merchant to arrive in Oporto was John Croft who came in 1678, and the Croft name became the most respected among those who subsequently came to join the wine trade. But of course what Croft would have been shipping was Blackstrap. Fortified Port wine, as we know it, was quite a few generations in the future. That same year a Liverpool wine importer sent his two sons to Oporto to learn about wine growing and making. There were better wine areas in Europe for learning the trade but he sent them to Portugal and Oporto. At Lamego in the High Douro they found a monastery that grew wine and an Abbot with ideas. During fermentation, but before it was completed, he added brandy which killed the yeast, which halted fermentation to give a sweet, highly alcoholic table wine. They might have been the first Englishmen to taste the precursor of Port wine, in that year of 1678. What they did with the knowledge is not recorded. How they ever penetrated to the High Douro at that time might have been even more interesting, and it is doubtful if what they tasted bore much resemblance to the wines of 100 years later. Before very long, gradually the English and Scottish made the arduous route to Lisbon and Oporto, intent on becoming traders; and then merchants, a notch or two up the social scale. In the course of a generation or two through hard work and an intelligent appreciation of what was required to make the Douro wine industry one that could be launched into a market greater in every way than the indigenous natives could have imagined, a commendable industry emerged. Ultimately some of the merchants grew very rich and grand. Not quite in the style of the East Indian Company grandees with its own army though of the same period, but grand enough. Dynasties were created; and today despite take-overs, 18th and 19th century names of the original courageous merchants are not difficult to find. Sandeman, Symington, Dow, Taylor, Graham and Cockburn Port wines will be found on all good supermarket shelves.

Portugal was never a colony but one has the feeling that some merchants in a subtle way may have considered their hosts as "Lesser breeds without the law" to quote Kipling. The sort that was sure that God must be an Englishman and a Protestant one at that. The devout Portuguese might on occasions have cast a jaundiced eye on some of the Anglo-Saxon practices and the Inquisition still in Portugal, an authority of great power in the 19th century, would have sent these "heretical devils" packing had it been politically possible. The relationship between the Port wine expatriates with the local people seems to have been quite different to that of the Claret expatriates in Bordeaux and the Sherry Expatriates in Jerez; where quite quickly there was intermarriage with local families, despite religious differences. This does not seem to have been the case in Oporto; and one wonders why.

By 1800 there were more than 100 members of the British Association of Port Shippers and the social headquarters of this important group was the splendid Factory House. It was considered to be an exclusive men's club and, as such, it is well into its third century.

The River Douro is a savage, beautiful river. It rises in Spain not far from Rioja, but over the Portuguese border it dives into a deep gorge, nearly all the way until it reaches the sea at Oporto. The wine lodges in Vila Nova da Gaia are 50 miles from the wild and beautiful country where the grapes are grown. When the English merchants first saw the land, which was to become the source of their wealth, they would have been shaken by the primitive lives of the peasants. It is unlikely the roads of Portugal in the 16th, 17th and 18th centuries were better than the French and it must have been daunting for the urbanites of Oporto to go up country, and how did the wine get to Oporto? I recall a story which said that the barrels were rolled into the river and somehow or other reached Oporto.

The area of wine cultivation was about 75,000 acres and about 30,000 growers, whose sole income came from grapes. That gave each grower about 2 acres each. But there were 80,000 vineyard sites, meaning a grower might be working on more than one site to make up his two acres; which was very hard work indeed for the seven pennies a day he was paid in 1850, and a pipe of wine was sold for between 15 shillings and three pounds. The peasants were not so much peasants as serfs; tied to the land with all that implied; at least until well into the twentieth century; and life for them had not changed much in many generations.

I was first in Portugal in 1952. The road from Lisbon to Oporto was quite fair and the entrance to the town over the high bridge spanning the river dramatic. On the left could be seen the factories and lodges of the shippers with the names emblazoned in big letters, Cockburn, Taylor, Graham, Sandeman, Dow, Warre and Delaforce. My agent was with me and made a far from new joke. "The best road in Oporto" he said "is the one back to Lisbon." Later I saw his point. It was distasteful to see streets crammed with men spitting on the pavement; not a woman in sight, nor in the cafés. Where were the women? The churches were as crammed with women as the streets were with men. Education was only compulsory up to the age of 12; and the further you went from Lisbon you met children who had been working from the age of 10. Portugal had many large estates owned by relatively few people, and in the Douro I doubt if many of the vineyard workers owned any land, though some would have been tenants. Even when the co-operatives were formed, the members would have been tenants of the land-owners who, with Governmental nods and winks, could always call the tune. Memories are short; people forget that until Salazar's death in 1970 and the Revolution of 1974 there had never been as much as a whiff of democracy in Portugal.

This question of strength, which turns a powerful and far from pleasant red table wine into Port wine and when it was first done, does not seem to have an answer. My belief is it may almost have been accidental. Firstly the nasty, hard tannic taste was softened by retaining some unfermented grape sugar, then adding about 3% of brandy. This brew would then be enjoyed by those, especially women, who liked the effect of alcohol but not the taste. Men would like it because it was an unusually powerful table wine. That is perhaps how Blackstrap was born. Later, somebody experimented with the quantity of brandy added, and the result was a luscious dessert wine called Port. But the evidence suggests it may have taken place over possibly 60 years, and may have been linked to excise duties payable on entry to the UK. Blackstrap probably had about 3 gallons of brandy added to a pipe (a pipe was anything between 110 and 130 gallons). To many drinkers in the UK this was ideal, when wars denied entry of French wines. A wine that was like a good Burgundy. Little did they know that a "good" Burgundy was also doctored with more highly alcoholic wines from Southern Countries. It seems that authentic Port wine consisting of an inclusion of 20% to 25% of brandy was possibly not regularly available until the middle of the 19th century.

I also read that the propagation of this view won you few friends among the Oporto shippers; boat rockers are never popular. To give an idea of the influence of British merchants, there was an area of the Alto Douro, which had the best regarded vineyards, set-aside solely for making Port wine for shipment to the UK and classified as the 1st quality.

The description "Port wine" was in general used by the mid-18th century and Christie's first used it in a catalogue in 1708; but the reference was always to red wine. Clearly using the word "Port" identified where the wine came from, not its nature. By the early 19th century, importers were still asking the shippers "to go easy" on the brandy "we want a wine to be like a Burgundy" which, apart from anything else might include a discreet dose of the excellent "marc de

Bourgogne" which the Burgundian vigneron distils yearly from the skins and stalks after the vintage. It gives him a nice little Winter job, and extra income.

# 14

# THE CRITICAL PATH OF THE PORT WINE MAN (OR, FROM LONDON TO OPORTO AND BACK)

How did you become a merchant and shipper of Port wine in the 18th and 19th century? I am assuming you were not Portuguese, but probably Anglo-Saxon English or a Scot. Perhaps a Huguenot; a French Protestant whose ancestors had fled France after the Revocation of the Treaty of Nantes in 1685, which led to the wholesale massacre of Huguenots in Paris and other parts of France. As did the Jews later, the Huguenots enriched the quality of life in England and Ireland by their contribution to engineering, banking business and the arts. The Delaforce family were Huguenots and one of the most successful shippers in Oporto.

Sources of credit were rare and unreliable; the monetary system primitive and until the beginning of the 18th century, no paper money. Thus anyone who wanted to start a business requiring capital would have trouble raising it, and the only source was family or friends. Perhaps young George Sandeman, whose family for many years was the greatest name in the Oporto business was typical, but perhaps he was just lucky. Though in my experience luck in business goes to those who deserve it most. George's father lent him £300, a huge sum in 1790 to set-up as a wine importer in London. The family was Scottish from Perth, and his father must have been a good judge of character to have advanced such a sum to a young man aged 26. If you were educated and of a respectable family, you could look around the mercantile section of the City of London, and find an importer prepared to take you on as an unpaid apprentice for perhaps £25 a year. You might gain a couple of years valuable training in business, book-keeping, debt collecting and a knowledge of human nature, particularly the shady part. If you were exceptionally smart you would also disbelieve half the chat and rumours you heard and have strong doubts of the other half. I am assuming you would be a man in his early twenties, and not wet behind the ears. You would probably have stored a mass of useful information and got to know people in Portugal who were part of the wine industry. So when you left London for Oporto you would have a good idea of the tasks that lay ahead, and knowledge of the London end of the trade. You would in fact have carried out what is called today "networking", which would be of incalculable value and the basis of your future and fortune. You might also have been invited to join the Masonic Order; and that would certainly not have done you any harm. It certainly did none to at least six of the first thirteen Presidents of America, including George Washington, who were Masons.

You would have learnt that the quickest way to make money was to sell things, not make them. Buy wine and sell it to a London importer. Most important keep well away, for the moment, from growing wine or holding huge stocks, for these were perilous pursuits for the unwary, the unlucky or foolish.

So now your contacts have got you employment with an Oporto shipper or merchant; probably on a small salary but enough to live on in a country where living was cheap; and after a couple of years or so the possessor of enough experience and business contacts to go back to London and set-up as an importer. People would know you and have confidence in you. More hard work would lie ahead, but at least you would learn whether or not you could cut the mustard in the importing game, perhaps dealing in other goods as well. Then if you knew a few of the right people you might tackle the most arduous task of all, climbing the greasy pole to join the Great and the Good of the City of London at the top tables. After all, Dick Whittington did it, but if you were a really adventurous cove you might decide to go back to Oporto. You were a prosperous importer and had made enough money to expand into shipping. You also had agents in Dublin, Bristol and Edinburgh. You would remember the climate, the balmy Springs and the splendid Summers; the low cost of living and the cheapness of servants which your wife would like, and it is always easier to be a big fish in a small pond.

All this sounds like the perfect dream, but something along these lines must have been taking intrepid young men abroad to make their fortune. It only needed a little money, and luck, and lots of courage. Well if you took this Critical Path (another Business School mantra) and returned to Oporto, set-up your shipping company, bought or built a lodge in Vila Nova da Gaia for the storage and ageing of the wine, you might decide to take the tricky road to the Upper Douro and buy a vineyard or a share of one. You could take such a risk now, having made a lot of money in London where your importing firm was still strong and would guarantee a regular supply of wine to fill your lodge in Vila Nova da Gaia. So now the circle was complete. You owned the vineyard, you were the shipper, the importer, and perhaps owned some of the retail outlets, and avoided just being a grower, at the mercy of brokers, shippers and importers.

# 15

# THE FACTORY HOUSE

In the period 1800–1990, the Factory House, as it was called had 94 members. Only 9 of these were members post 1900 and all were merchants or Port wine shippers. Hunt Roope were trading from 1730. The names we have known for years and still remember are on the list, Cockburn, Croft, Delaforce, Gonzales, Byass, Graham, Offley Forester, Sandeman, Taylor, Warre. Symington's came rather late in the 19th century but is still a family firm, and bought up many of the older shippers. The others were well known in their day, then were absorbed by larger shippers. Then most of the big shippers ended-up as part of huge conglomerates. The predators were always smart enough to recognise the value of a name brand and have kept the great names alive. All-in-all the British expatriates who made the brave decision to take their chances in a foreign land speaking a different language, firstly in the late 17th century, were blood brothers who did the same in Bordeaux, Jerez, Madeira, Cognac and Marsala. They were certainly not like the robber barons who pacified South Africa, Kenya and other parts of that unhappy continent of Africa. They made their mark by hard work, business skill and force of character, and were always a minority within a majority of Dutch, French, German and others. But of this polyglot group that worked in the Port wine trade, the name that is recognised above others and is synonymous with Port is England.

The Factory House is an anachronism but is as

significant as the Tate Modern Art Gallery and may last a lot longer. For it is a living edifice of bricks and mortar that is strangely organic, still working, a monument to a small number of expatriate Anglo-Saxons who created a product, Port wine in a friendly foreign country called Portugal, that for over 200 years is still to be found or drank in the sitting rooms or dining rooms of half the world.

From at least 1642 when Nicholas Comerforde was British Consul in Lisbon, there have been British traders in Portugal. A consul was usually appointed to protect the interests of British people domiciled in a foreign country, and the people protected were usually merchants and their families. These people would usually live close together, and meet in a private house to discuss business and other matters. Wherever they were, the place was called the British Factory, though nothing was made there except perhaps money.

In Oporto and after much talk and delay, the merchants all in the wine trade, financed, commissioned a British architect to design a building to be called the Factory House. Started in 1785, it was finished in 1790. At the same time the Oporto town council granted permission to the merchants to buy land for a British Cemetery for the burial of "English vassals". Nicely put, indicating the expatriates were only guests in Oporto, but the cemetery had to be situated outside the town walls so that its presence would not offend the devout Catholic people, who did not like dead heretics any more than live ones.

The Factory House along with the British Cemetery and later the Oporto Cricket Club, to be visited in due course by many famous amateur clubs such as the MCC, Dorset Rangers, Eton Ramblers, Gentlemen of Worcester and the Law Society, gave the British a feeling of belonging. They worshipped Mammon in the Factory House, the Protestant

God in the English Chapel and were buried by a Church of England Clergyman in the British Cemetery. What absolute bliss. The Factory House on a corner of the fittingly named Rua dos Inglezes stands prominent, though not like a sore thumb, close to the Douro River. It is grand, like the Carlton, or the Liberal Club in Whitehall. Any member of the British Aristocracy would have felt at home in it, and many came. Its interior was classical English with its capacious drawing room, dining room, map room, ballroom, billiards room, smoking room, writing room and other rooms too numerous to remember; all to give the members a feeling that for a while they were back home.

It was run like a very exclusive London gentleman's club; which of course was the intention, and in the early years Portuguese people were not invited, though as employees they were welcome as well as necessary, and no doubt ran the place like clockwork as did the Sergeants in a good British regiment. After a few years male Portuguese of the better sort were invited to dinner or to luncheon; but no officers below Field Rank, that is "major". The careful selection must have gone down like a lead balloon to the Portuguese, thousands of whom were fighting with Wellington to repel the French and expel them from Spain. They fought bravely throughout the Peninsular War, notably at the siege of Badejoz. They were present to relieve the siege of Oporto in 1809. Vila Nova da Gaia had a lucky escape. Nobody told the British soldiery of the sea of wine in the Lodges. Had they known of it, even Wellington's threat of the gallows would not have got them out.

No members' wives were allowed to dine in the Factory House until August 1843, as this was the ultimate honour and rarely repeated. Balls put on for the King of Portugal in 1861 and 1863 got the ladies in, and Queen Elizabeth with

Prince Philip were received with great splendour in 1957, but the imprimatur was stamped on the Factory House when Margaret Thatcher was invited to dinner along with Dr Mario Soares, the Portuguese Prime Minister in April 1984. Little changed though in the 140 years between the ladies luncheon in 1843 and now. Though every 3 months or so, at least until about 2000 there were mixed sex luncheons.

The way of life in Oporto and Vila Nova de Gaia was so different to that on the Quai des Chartrons and its people, the Chartronnais in Bordeaux. Less louche perhaps, a more uptight attitude to the Portuguese than that between the Chartronnais and the French, but they were of the same bones and sinews of the expatriates in the Medoc. Maybe they needed a few Anglo Irish to lighten things up, or some Catholic Irish ex- soldiers who had fought for the French in the Irish Brigade against the English.

I was again in Oporto on business in November 1961, and by an arrangement made in London, I was entertained by a young member of the Graham Family in their Vila Nova da Gaia lodge. We sampled our first port at about 11 o'clock in the morning, and with an interlude for lunch, our last at about 4 in the afternoon, which, for all I knew, was creosote; everything was a blank by then! But I learnt more about Port wine that day than in the rest of my life.

# 16

# MADEIRA

*(Wanted, sturdy fellow to work in Funchal wine lodge, must be strong swimmer)*

Most islands within the general orbit of Europe have a history of sorts earlier than the beginning of the foundation of Rome, put at 753 BC. Which, one might say, was early enough. But Madeira? Nothing, a blank. Somebody must have landed there if only to have a look around; and I suspect Berbers, sometime after the warriors of Islam, sword in one hand, the Koran in the other, reached the Atlantic coast of modern Morocco, not long after the invasion of Spain which began in 710. Though the Phoenicians were there in the 5th century BC. Madeira is only 400 miles off the coast. Raiders must have viewed the formidable cliffs from time to time; but if a landing *was* made and a settlement established, there was no evidence of this when a known landing was decided upon.

In 1419 the Portuguese sea captain João Goncalvez known as "the Crossed-Eyed" alias Zarco. Cross-eyed or not he was certainly cross, for he set the place alight as it was heavily wooded and not suited for agriculture. History says it was 7 years before the fire burnt itself out. How on earth did the fire last 7 years? Zarco must have been the world's greatest ever arsonist, beating Nero into a cocked hat! Whenever I try to coerce a woodpile in my garden into flames, it gives up the ghost within an hour.

A lot of rain falls on Madeira, which makes a 7-year fire surprising but however long the end result was greatly beneficial. The potash and other elements in the wood ashes provided a well-fertilised soil for many crops including grapes.

A few years later, a colonising expedition arrived from Portugal led by Zarco. Mostly Portuguese of course but as usual included a pot pouri of foreign adventurers and a Scot, John Drummond. Zarco was made Governor of the island and held the post for 40 years, during which time the land was planted with wheat, maize and vines; sugar also which later was to become a very important source of alcohol for the wine industry. Though I doubt its presence during those pre-wine days. Sugar came first to Europe from India and other places further East. Ferdinand Magellan did not circumnavigate the Earth until 1519 and was dead in 1521, though one of his ships that reached home may have had seeds of the sugarcane on board, but this would have been more than 100 years after Zarco's settlement.

A distinctive feature of Portugal's massive program of colonisation was to flood each place taken over with unlettered, very poor peasants from the mother country, and not always of their own free will. This they did in all their African possessions and in Macao.

There was never a substantial middle-class in Portugal, and over the generations of colonial exploitation few were prepared to leave the comforts of Lisbon and other towns for the wilds of Africa, the discomforts and disease. Unless, of course, in positions of authority which carried with it rank and position. Of the colonies only Brazil became outstandingly prosperous and by 1800 had outstripped Portugal in prosperity. Portugal remained poor until well into the 20th century, and certainly had no cash to spend in Madeira,

Angola or Mozambique. In none of those places did the building of roads rank highly in budget priority; nor for that matter in Portugal. In Madeira roads were so bad even between the two World Wars that wheeled conveyances of any sort were scarce, and the principal means of moving goods was by horse-drawn, or even man-drawn sledges skidding over the cobbles of Funchal and the few other towns. People were sometimes carried in a type of sedan chair. Now, a pipe or barrel of wine, a Madeiran pipe, ie. 90–100 gallons weighs perhaps 900 lbs. In the absence of the wheel, and a barrel being round shaped, it began its export life by being rolled down the cobbled streets of Funchal to the waters edge and into the sea, at which point the "sturdy fellow" referred to in the sub-title of this chapter, jumped into the sea and pushed the pipe of wine through the water to the cargo ship at anchor offshore, because Funchal had no mole, jetty or breakwater to form a harbour. Madeira is hardly bigger than the Isle of Man, and with many streams leading down to the sea, the best way of getting to one point or another was by small boat.

It is clear, and the history is accurate enough to believe that the island has been making wine by primitive means since the late 15th century and despite its lack of a proper harbour it became a regular port of call for the considerable number of vessels from the 16th century going East to India and the Far East, to take on water, fresh food and since it was available, wine. So wine was not so much exported as taken away by the customer. It was a buyers not a sellers market. At this time the principal customers were the Dutch who bought wine en route to the Dutch East Indies. Or, of course, the Netherlands on the way back. The ships were part of the commercial fleet owned by the Dutch East India Company formed in 1602, principally to trade in spices.

Cloves, nutmegs and mace could form a cargo worth a king's ransom. The English East India Company fought the Dutch fiercely to win part of the spice trade. Cane sugar was now grown, so alcohol was available for adding to the wine to stablise it during the long sea voyage and as a palatable rum-type of drink for the wine growers. Alcohol, whether made from sugarcane or distilled from wine does wonders for a fermented wine when two to three % is added. It gives depth and body to a wine with only 10 degrees, and on a long sea voyage keeps it well away from its ultimate fate of becoming vinegar.

I first saw the island in January 1976 and the impression was favourable. A climate that was equable, no seasons as we know them farther North; lots of bananas and indifferent wines from which exquisite dessert wines was made. It was also chock-a-block with Anglo-Saxon expatriates, some of them 5th or 6th generation who like those in Oporto, Jerez and Bordeaux took the faltering business of the locals and turned it into an international one.

# 17

# MADEIRA: THE MAKING OF THE WINE

High temperature in wine can be a near disaster, which is why the availability of refrigeration in hot climates such as the South of France, Southern Italy and Spain turned indifferent whites, oxidised, lacking acid and finesse into excellent whites, which you might think worth of Alsace, the Rheingau or the Mosel, hundreds of miles to the North, but with Madeira in some magical way extreme heat (40°-50° c) is used to turn a poor base wine into something which in 18th/19th century England usurped Port as "the Englishman's wine": for a time anyway.

The best Madeira's are made from four grapes called pretentiously "noble". They are all white and the names are Malvasia, Bual, Verdelho and Sercial. After pressing, the first three are fermented but the fermentation is halted early on by the addition of raw alcohol made from sugarcane, so that most of the grape sugar is retained. But the juice of the Sercial is completely fermented to an absolutely dry wine then fortified to give a total of 17-18°. For want of a better description the result is something like a very dry sherry, but would be considered to be a table wine. When later the actual wine making was taken away from the tiny vineyards, mostly less than an acre, to Funchal some miles away, the unfermented juice was transported in goatskins called barrachos. The weight of 40 to 50 litres was carried on the back of a peasant to the winemaking point. The only other work I can think of to approach this in severity is that endured by a miner at the coalface. The Durham miner blacked by coal, the peasant in Madeira blackened by the sun. They were soul mates in adversity. The sweet wine with an alcoholic content of 20–25° was very popular in England because it had all the attractive features of Port, and it was this dessert wine that the ships going East to India and the East Indies, and West to America especially to South Carolina and Boston delivered to eagerly awaiting customers. It gave them that marvellous comfortable feeling of well-being, what the Germans call "gemutlichkeit"; comfort before oblivion!

# 18

# MADEIRA AFTER THE RETURN OF CHARLES II IN 1662

The marriage of Charles II to the Portuguese princess, Catherine of Braganza in 1662, was important for England and English trade. As a dowry Charles received Bombay, tremendously important as history proved, and Tangier. The latter was abandoned, as with Gibraltar to guard the Straits when captured from Spain in 1703, was not thereafter required. This alliance with Portugal also gave us influence in Madeira with its shipping routes to the West and South; and by 1680 of the 25 shipping companies despatching wine from Funchal, the majority of the foreign traders were English. A Consul was in place since 1658, though a Dutch Consul had been there for many years before.

The name William Bolton is historically important in the developing of the wine industry. He came in 1695, representing Robert Heysham, a merchant banker and Alderman of the City of London. He shipped wine to Heysham's brother in Barbados, and to Boston, in large quantities. Bolton's true value was his infinite capacity to write letters mainly to Heysham which revealed his character and told for posterity the story of the Anglo-Saxon penetration of Madeira; its way of life and work. His letters to Heysham reveal a man that was sarcastic, irascible, demanding, who never became reconciled to living abroad; though he stayed save a brief absence until sometime in the 1720's. The Bolton letters are famous and secure for posterity. He was already

46 when he reached the island. A younger man less hardened in his ways and views, not so much a "God damn you Sir" Englishman might have painted another picture. Bolton can claim the reportage of an important development in wine making when he went home on a brief visit. Two men, Durrell and Morgan, with whom he wanted to form a company, were making brandy distilled from the local wine and using it as a fortifying medium. The wine that was to become the famous dessert wine Madeira now had a total alcohol of 20–25° but whether or not he was actually reporting an addition of 2–3° of brandy to make a version of Oporto Blackstrap or the larger percentage to make a sort of Port wine is not clear. If it was the latter then Durrell and Morgan were many years in advance of what the Oporto shippers did to make Port wine.

What separates Madeira from all other wines is its ability to change its taste and nature after the exposure to extreme heat and violent pitching and tossing during a long sea voyage. No other wine ever received such harsh treatment. The general view of wine makers everywhere was that such treatment could only damage, not improve. But the information of change and improvement could only have come from customers, and the shippers in Funchal would have been foolish to ignore it. The feedback received could hardly be ignored when it said that the wine after the long sea trip had softened, mellowed such as could normally be achieved only after some years in cask and bottle. Whatever caused the change it was the Anglo-Saxon shippers now making their presence felt that initiated the program of artificially creating the conditions in the wine lodge *before* shipment, that the wine endured during the sea voyage. Firstly they assumed that heat that was the principal cause of change. Beginning in the late 18th and early 19th centuries the lodges built *estufagem*, heating rooms. The pipes of wine were lined up in these, and under-floor furnaces of wood or coal provided the heat by radiation to the pipes. This early primitive system was difficult to control, but largely it did what was needed until water pipes filled with steam or hot water could be fitted inside the rooms complete with heat control instruments. The wine was subjected to heat for about 90 days, during which time the wine could be tasted to observe change, and this more or less is the practice of today's wine makers. Alternatively the pipes or casks are kept in sealed rooms in which wet steam is circulated as the heat source.

For the better and more expensive wines, another system altogether is used. The pipes are laid out in the top rooms of the lodge which had glass roofs to admit the sun which would provide heat for most of the year as required but a more gentle heat in which the wine might be held for several years, during which time a degree of oxygen penetrates into the pipe, as it does through the cork in a bottle of old Claret. This treatment gives stability and longevity, and an opened bottle might still be drinkable after 6 years, or in a closed, unopened bottle after 100 years. In the Southern States of America where cellars for many reasons were difficult to build the ability for the wine to be stored above ground in hot summers was greatly prized.

# 19

# THE EXPATRIATES OF MADEIRA

Six names were to dominate the Madeira wine trade, and push it out to the great markets of England and elsewhere, especially the colonies where the English language was spoken. John Leacock came in 1745; Francis Newton in 1748 and both founded dynasties that survived at least until the 1960's. John Blandy, born in Dorchester in 1783, came to the island with General Beresford's division in about 1810. He was Beresford's quartermaster in the Army; very good training for success in business. William Cossart came in 1808. William Grant arrived from Nairn in 1803, and with Rutherford, another Scot, formed Rutherford and Grant Company in 1810. All these were shippers and wine makers. Like those who had gone to Oporto, Jerez and Bordeaux, almost to a man they were Protestants.

**LEACOCK** John: came at 15 to be apprenticed to a Madeiran merchant, Catanach & Murdoch. He served his 7 years, received his indentures, remained with the firm and married Murdoch's daughter. A very popular way to reach the top of a company. There is an Anglo-Saxon expression that aptly describes this route to the top, but I won't repeat it. Leacock seems to have drifted from general trading to making and shipping wine, but he prospered, and sons were brought into the business. He died in 1899 at the age of 74, after 59 years on the island, and the Firm continues to trade as

Leacock and Company.

**NEWTON** Francis: a young Scot, reached Madeira after a somewhat circuitous route. Thought to have been a survivor of Bonny Prince Charlie's '45 Rebellion. Though, as a Protestant, he would hardly have been fighting on the Catholic side. On the other hand, as a Catholic, it would have been a good time to escape from England. This he did, going to Flanders to do some soldiering but he came of a good family and after Flanders he got a job in St Kitts in the West Indies as an overseer on a plantation which would have given him experience in handling labour – slave labour. He was offered £100 to stay on but refused and sailed to Madeira, arriving in 1748. I suspect he had influence through his family as he got a good bookkeeping job with José da Camara, a descendant of Zarco the Founder of the Island and a big estate owner. Newton had freedom to trade on his own account, setting off on the road to wealth. He wrote to a friend saying:

> *"The only disadvantages one has here, there are no recreations, diversions or companions. The Portuguese are a very proud, deceitful people and, in short, there is no such thing as finding one a companion as very few of them have good education unless the Priests or Collegians, whose ceremonies are so many and conversation is so disagreeable. As for the English here, they are much worse, there is nothing but jealousy of one another's correspondents, everybody trying all he can to get anothers, that they scarcely speak to one another."*

Broadly speaking what he meant was "the locals are all Catholics, bigoted and unpleasant. The English are boring and ignorant oiks, and there are no women." He could have added "there is nothing to do but work and make money." Which is precisely what he did, the other merchants also. He and Leacock were not particularly friendly. Possibly he thought Leacock came up through the ranks. But they did work together to create the first organised shipping and wine making company on Madeira. Co-operation with others laid the foundations of a great industry. Newton also talked about mastering the language, which even today, much less than then is a very un-British thing to do. Both were very enterprising and continued to import and export a variety of produce. I recall meeting John Blandy in 1956 in Lisbon. He was there on company engineering business. At that time I did not know the position he held in the wine trade. It shows the sort of men these ex-pats were; nothing if not entrepreneurial.

**BLANDY** John: Not long after arriving on the island with the Army, he went home, collected a wife, Janet Burden, returned to the island to spend the rest of his life in the services of wine; an honourable trade with a long history. His son, Charles Ridpath Blandy, lived until 1870; his grandson, John Burden Blandy until 1912; his great grandson, John Ernest until 1930, while his great, great grandsons, Graham and John, continued the dynasty until the end of the 20th century and there are Blandys still active in the trade that has rightly brought great reward to the family.

I have always admired dynasties in industry, especially in the ancient trades. My own profession is old, perhaps as old as the vine, and I never forget that piece of wisdom written by a 17th century ironmaster:

*"Iron seemeth a simple metal*
*But in its nature are many mysteries*

*And men that bend them to their minds*
*Shall, in arriving days*
*Gather therefrom great profit*
*Not for them alone but for all mankind."*

An illustrious adjunct to the family was the great Victorian, William Thompson, later Lord Kelvin, the Scottish mathematician and physicist whose works on electrostatics made possible the laying of the Atlantic submarine communication cables. He came to Madeira while working on this project, and married Fanny Blandy in 1874 in the English Church in Funchal. He married her, he said, because she was the only person on the island who understood what he was talking about.

**BLANDY** John Burden (father of JE): provided another example of Blandy enterprise and foresight when in 1894 he launched a coastal steamer called Falcao; the first of several. JB complained that the priests tried to forbid their flocks from using the Falcao and to use the S. Joao, a Catholic boat instead. John Ernest Blandy made his name when in 1896 he had a Spanish ship seized in Le Havre, which was carrying a cargo of fake Madeira labelled "vin de Madère." He got an order from the French Court, which allowed him to take the cargo of 500 pipes and presumably destroy it. This was a fine example of hard-nosed Protestantism, protecting its interests and is further proof of the success of these tough ex-pats like the Blandys.

**COSSART** William: The first of the Cossarts arrived on the island in 1808. An Anglo-Irishman of Hugenot stock, whose family had been in Ireland for 100 years, he left Dublin in 1802 and his ship was taken by the French, but

1802 was the year of the Amiens Peace Treaty, a welcome break in the Napoleonic War. So what was he doing between 1802 and 1808? He joined the firm founded by Francis Newton, then called Newton Gordon Murdoch and Scott, and his nephew also joined him. There were other Cossarts, Layland, Noel, Arthur, David and there has never lacked a Cossart in the Madeira wine industry until the present day. The present firm of Cossart Gordon contains no fewer than five members of the family.

# 20

# THE YEARS FROM 1920 TO THE 21ST CENTURY

There was a massive turndown in business caused by the passing of the Volstead Act in the USA, which lasted until 1932 when Roosevelt got rid of it. It had done nothing for the economy, increased crime, gave the Mafia many recruits and made the Kennedy family super-rich through its liquor smuggling activities and corruption. The loss of the Russian business in 1917 was terrible. There was a recovery in trade with America after 1932; and unexpectedly Scandinavia turned-up trumps. In 1939 Denmark, it is said, bought 30% of the entire wine output, and Sweden became a big drinker of Madeira wine. But social habits changed; the mid-morning pick-me-up disappeared in the UK, and the afternoon glass of Malvasia with a slice of cake also. Sherry had become more popular among the middle classes, usually what was called brown sherry, meaning a dark coloured liquid of cloying sweetness and not in the same league as a Malvasia or a Bual. The huge successes of the late 18th/19th centuries when Madeira from time to time sold better than Port or Sherry, or even Claret, were not to be repeated. Though the best Madeiras had a steady market especially the dryer Sercial and Verdelho. The dessert wines seem out of fashion; though not in Continental Europe. People often confuse the dryer wines with Sherry and the dessert wines with Port, but the styles are quite different. Not better, nor inferior but different. As with many products, cars, machine tools, classic brands of clothes, whisky and great Claret growths, the rapidly growing markets of China and India offer huge possibilities for the wines of the lovely island of Madeira, and I foresee great sales especially in China, and a fine future for the descendents of the Newton, Leacocks, Blandys, Cossarts and others.

The Madeira Wine Company is the largest producer on the island. It began in 1913 as the Madeira Wine Association, when Welsh & Cunha along with Henriques & Camara, came together. Other companies in difficulty joined in 1925, and Blandys with their interests in shipping and tourism, started to flex their muscles and took a leading role. John Blandy became the first chairman in the enlarged Association. Other famous names recognising the new problems ahead in a rapidly changing market also joined, Rutherford & Miles and Cossart Gordon. Twenty seven wine houses had now joined the Association and the name was changed to the Madeira Wine Company, and together they account for about 40% of the wine exports, mostly shipped by Blandy, Cossart, Leacock and Miles.

The Company works in two Lodges in Funchal's centre. The São Francisco Lodge housed in an old monastery next to the tourist office on the Avenida Arriaga, is open to visitors as a useful public relations exercise. Above, under the roofs, wooden attics house *canteirus* of old wines ageing slowly in sub-tropical heat, and they are the best. Casks of American oak store 70,000 litres, while downstairs a dusty vino theque contains 50,000 bottles of vintage Madeiras.

The Company maintains the "house styles", a difficult task but done, and the best are bottled under the Blandy, Cossart and Gordon labels. Stocks of vintage wines are to be seen dating back to 1822.

The Madeira Wine Company does not stand still; not since the 1974 revolution which shook the island as it did in

Portugal. There were further changes when the Leacocks sold their shares in the Company to the Blandys. And in 1988 it went public and the Symington family of Dow, Graham and Warre, the greatest names in the Port business bought a 46% stake in the Company, which made them equal partners with Blandy Brothers. This, and an ultra-modern approach to business have assured the future for Madeira wines.

The contact with native Madeirans until probably the mid-20th century was probably remote except for business. Like all small communities and islands would be typical, the locals, especially at the lower end of the social scale put up barriers against association with non-Catholics. The influence of the priest was strong, in particular among the women. Less so among the educated classes, but with no industry or work other than in agriculture, anybody with education would be likely to move to Portugal, or other places. I have little reliable information on relationships leading to marriages between Protestants and Catholics but the barriers erected by both communities would have been formidable. Leacocks and Cossarts, Blandys and Newtons produced many siblings and there were plenty of marriages between the expatriate families. There was no "fishing fleet" as it was called in India during the Raj, when scores of demure, well brought-up young ladies, all unmarried, terrified of being left on the shelf, sailed into Bombay, Madras and Calcutta each year, hoping to find a husband among the thousands of slightly elderly, unmarried Anglo-Saxon men, somewhat sex-starved and not too choosy. Marriage was a necessity if the firm was to continue to the next and successive generations, and in one way or another the job was done, and after 250 years or more, the old names are there for all to see on the bottle labels.

For those visitors or travellers shrewd enough to choose Madeira for a holiday, they will be in a climate that is an absolute joy from the first day of January to the last day of December. Rain but not too much, hardly more than that necessary to lay the dust. Sun, but not the torrid heat of Africa, which is quite close; and nearly every day. Possibly the best climate in the world; unless you are a Winter sports freak!

Whether you are Protestant, Catholic or atheist, I suggest you attend the 11 o'clock service on a Sunday morning, where you will see, may even meet, wine shippers and their families. The church will be full, the hymns familiar, the voices perhaps wavering a little, but backed-up by more than a few of the younger members of the congregation (perhaps the next generation of wine makers and shippers). It will be like being in a 12th century Norman church in an ancient English village. And with the fading of the last rousing hymn, you may feel that a glass or two of a splendid Malvasia or Sercial would be a good start to another enjoyable week.

In a slightly more sombre mood, and before the walk to the wine bar, seek out the Protestant Cemetery, and read the headstones. In the 19th century many families in the UK with young members suffering from tuberculosis, sought a cure for them in the warm climate of Madeira. Many young people between the ages of 15 and 21 arrived only to die shortly after as the headstones show; for at the time there was no cure for TB. The headstones also tell something of the Anglo-Saxon expatriates who came to work, to live and to die.

Then when you get home, and the next time you are in London, go to Villiers Street, which leads up from the Embankment tube towards the Strand, and risking a broken ankle or perhaps a leg descend the rickety staircase to Gordon's Wine Bar. This was the first to get a licence in the 19th century and was bought by Luiz Gordon (no relation) in 1970, and looks and probably is unreconstructed for about 100 years. There, direct from the wood, you can buy at reasonable prices, a splendid glass of Madeira, or Port or Sherry; and the food also is not half bad. Luiz was, for sadly he died in 2002, of the Gordon family that turned-up in Jerez in 1756 to make a living out of the Sherry trade. The regulars still turn-up, usually at lunchtime, to drink a toast to Luiz.

# 21

## MARSALA

When the Sicilian Vespers signalled the massacre of the Norman French in 1282, the island had been growing wine for at least 1700 years. Madeira, when that vespers bell rang out, had to wait a further 127 years just to be discovered. Madeira, a small island hardly larger than the Isle of Man, and from a small start managed to sell to Georgian England a splendid wine that doubled as a dessert wine and as an aperitif/ table wine. Meanwhile Sicily, 34 times as big was still churning out wines of most appalling quality after more than 2000 years of experience. And it was not until about 40 years ago that decent whites and reds were made. But there was one place on the island that was different. Marsala, a small town and port on the extreme West coast which made a wine that attracted the attention of an English sea captain and merchant, who dropped his anchor there in 1773. He liked the wine and thought he could sell it in England, where a new alcoholic beverage always had a chance of a sale.

That man was John Woodhouse, and he considered the white wines of the area, grown in similar terroir and same hot sun had certain affinities with Sherry of which he had some knowledge. Now, whether or not the wine as made was blended with a small quantity of grape alcohol is unknown; but Woodhouse added about 2 gallons to each of 60 pipes of the wine. That is about 2% of the whole to give an overall alcohol content of about 18% and took them back home, to

London I suppose. Though Woodhouse was a Liverpool man, he had no difficulty in selling this large sample, which the customers found powerful and pleasant, especially the wealthy ones, who considered it as enjoyable as Sherry and Madeira, and in Regency and Victorian times frequently outsold both. This is nothing short of astonishing that in a handful of years, a fortified wine of no reputation should provide stiff and unexpected competition to the Sherry and Madeira importers. It soon became a snobbish and fashionable aperitif in the drawing rooms of Mayfair, Bath and Bristol, and the punters were demanding a regular supply. Now, here again, there is another of those mystifying gaps in time without explanation; as it was 1796, twenty three years later before Woodhouse returned to Marsala and established a wine blending centre near the fishing village of Cannozzo. Along with his sons, the Woodhouse Company was formed. Not much later, two other English families arrived, the Inghams and the Whittakers. They were, one supposes, competitors but with Marsala wine in vogue, and a ready market, their presence would have been welcomed by Woodhouse if only for company. The return in 1796 was opportune, as Nelson's large Navy became a good and regular customer. Marsala in the Officer's Mess, grog on the lower deck. There is an amusing apocryphal story, which has the ring of truth. Garibaldi, with his "Thousand" landed at Marsala in 1860 on his way to create the unification of all Italy; and because the British Navy was there taking wine on board, the Bourbon forces refrained from firing on Garibaldi's transports in case a British ship was damaged, and the wroth of England descended upon them.

 Sicily was and still is one of the largest wine growing provinces in Italy, but whereas the others make very palatable wines, Sicily continues to make rubbishy stuff save for a few very good wines for the table. Oddly, Sicilians are not thought to be big wine drinkers, though growing enormous volumes. This might explain poor viticulture, poor vine selection, carelessness in harvesting and wine making. On my first visit to Sicily in the 1950's (or rather the 2nd as I landed on the Syracuse beach on July 13th, 1943 on other business) there were precious few local wines that would have found a market North of Rome. Perhaps you might be in a good restaurant in, say, Palermo, eating a delicious plate of Frutta da Mare, or Gamberi alla cacciatore, only to have to wash it down with an allegedly white wine, amber-rust in colour, highly oxidised and alcohol topping 16°. The natural destination of most of Sicily's wines was either the Common Market wine lake for turning into industrial alcohol or for blending with low strength wines in other areas. Nevertheless, Sicily along with Puglia and Sardinia, remains the massive and still growing wine cellar of Europe. But Marsala for the best of reasons remains different. The British expatriates, and they were ex-pats in the best sense of the word, since they worked, lived and retired on the island, installed discipline, and encouraged viticultural skills among the wine growing peasantry.

CHANGES SINCE WOODHOUSE: The principal grape is the Grillo, which is the best, and is also grown in other parts of Sicily. The harvest is usually late picked, so is loaded with grape sugar and has a flavour called *rancio*. When pressed the must is fermented containing 16° of alcohol, a formidable level. One part of the pressing is made into table wine, another into *sifone*, which is a blend with semi-dried grapes and is slightly fortified with grape alcohol. There is also *cotto*, made from Catarratto grapes, boiled in a cauldron to be reduced to a heavy syrup, intensely sweet for adding to the base wine, to make a dessert wine, such as is known in England as "pudding wine", though it has neither the style nor the quality of the Sauternes. The very best is Marsala vergine, at least 5 years old, 18° of alcohol and dry. This is generally made by a system known as *lievite*, which can be compared to the Sherry Solera in its method of preparation.

There is a term in Italian wine law known as D.O.C. short for Denominazione di Origine Controllata. The Marsala area and those other places which supply the grapes are strictly D.O.C., which is as close a guarantee of probity as you are likely to get. It is not proof of quality but of honesty, and when you get honesty, in the end you may get quality as well. So the wines of Marsala whether sweet, very sweet, or dry, made to suit a particular market is an honest wine. I can think of wines from other places which are better known, cost much more, which are much less honest.

The great changes, almost a rebirth of Marsala wines took place when D.O.C., was introduced in 1969. It marked the road back to achieving a European reputation, and the prime mover was the Diego Rullo and Figli Company. It was that family company, founded in 1860 and worthy successors to John Woodhouse that finally, though much later, recovered World esteem for Marsala, created by John Woodhouse 100 years or more earlier. Florio is another family which came on the scene to rival Rullo and is now the largest producer.

Today it could be said that the Agnelli family, owners of FIAT, have inherited the Woodhouse legacy through the Florio Marsala Company, a subsidiary of Cinzano Vermouth Company, which is owned by FIAT. Taking an historical view, Marsala is an old wine that did not move out of puberty until an Englishman took it by the scruff of the neck to make it a worthy alternative to Madeira, Port or Sherry in England, and when it was taken-up by the sophisticated Milanese, Torinese and the lunch society of Rome, it was never going to look back. Sicily may have the Mafia but it also has Marsala.

# 22

# WINE FRAUDS DE NOS JOURS

*IPSWICH: THE WINE CAPITAL OF EAST ANGLIA.* It was not unknown two or three centuries ago that country wines such as parsnip or dandelion to be added to French imported wines not thought to be up to scratch. In the end the rich customers came to prefer the doctored wines to the original. That was not without its own particular irony, since most wines coming from Bordeaux had received treatment anyway. So when in 1966 wine importers working out of an Ipswich warehouse were, so to speak, caught with their trousers down by a diligent journalist, they were perhaps doing no more then resurrecting an old English practice of giving the customer what he wanted. How long this operation had been going on was not reported, but its Nemesis was Nick Tomalin, a journalist on the Sunday Times; and what a splendid story of fraud he and his team put together. Sadly Nick was killed in 1973 when reporting the Yom Kippur War between Israel and Egypt. What a pity it is that those whom the Gods love die young. Tomalin was a great loss to British journalism.

In this game of fraud, the label is King. No matter the shape of the bottle, much less what it contains, the Kings of Ipswich ruled like a cabal. There was Beaujolais King of Kings and his client Kings Nuit St Georges, St Emilion, Chateauneuf de Pape and St Julian. There was a firm in France called Société des Vin de France, which had a warehouse on the Ipswich harbour quay, well inland on the River

Orwell. Ipswich is a port with access to the North Sea. In the warehouse were the tools of the serious wine importer, tanks, hoses, pumps, bottling plant, and most important, an automatic labelling machine. This firm was a no nonsense supplier of vin ordinaire to French Families nationwide, who would buy it from the local grocer in one litre bottles labelled with the brand name Valpierre. The wine was red, a blend of Algerian, and wine from the Midi, both were cheap, and sold cheaply to the customers who expected nothing from it other than it was always on the table at mealtimes. The firm was dismayed that the British did not leap at the chance of drinking a cheap and cheerful sturdy French red at a low price even when the Revenue man had added his cut. At the time the per capita intake of wine in France was 150 bottles a year and in the UK 4 bottles. Not unreasonably they thought there was a huge market to exploit. Alas, after fighting the British on and off since the 13th century and only 26 miles of sea between the two, they had learnt nothing about their neighbour. Wine was a snob drink, drunk by the nobs, and what the Brits wanted was bottles with names they recognised, of which Beaujolais and Château du Pape led the small field. They lacked confidence in their own palates and wanted reassurance from a label. In the Kingdom of the blind the one-eyed man is King, and that man in his inanimate form of tanks, pumps and labelling machines was at hand on the quay at Ipswich.

The presence of this equipment came to Tomalin's attention in the Autumn of 1966, and he smelt a story. Then he was told that a small ship arrived in Ipswich several times a week, would turn-up at the quay and unload 550 gallon bulk containers of wine for pumping into the tanks in the warehouse. Tomalin was now like a dog with a bone, or perhaps a rat and set about collecting the evidence for exposing the fraud. Surprisingly the warehouse staff was very co-operative in giving details of the whole operation.

The French Company, seeing that their plan to sell vin ordinaire to the British *as* vin ordinaire was a failure, sold the complete installation to a merchant in Hertford, who had a mail order business to sell wine. He was already a customer of Vins de France Company, and had other ideas, which did not include selling vin ordinaire, at least not under the branch name of Valpierre. The plant manager was Michel Fontenoy; and he was good at his job. The tanks contained two basic reds; one called Vieux Pape (VP) and the other Eleven Five (ie. 11.5%). The VP was 12%. The system allowed the bottling plant to receive either wines, or a blend of both in whatever mix the client wanted and the label according to choice was automatically stuck on. The wholesale prices were astoundingly low.

*Beaujolais £5 a case*
*Châteauneuf du Pape £6.50 a case*

Mr Fontenoy was shocked that wine he was selling at ten shillings a gallon to the merchant was sold in restaurants at a mark-up of 1600 per cent!

When asked about his French reds, a spokesman for the merchant of the mail order firm said "I am pleased to offer these wines as good value and typical of their areas which I know well." *Where ignorance is bliss 'tis folly to be wise.*

A huge fraud was being committed on the public not in the wine so much as in the labels. The wine was pleasant enough, but was not as described on the label. But even if the restaurateurs did not know what they had bought, the wholesalers certainly did for they would have supplied the labels. But what matter? The end users, the drinkers, seemed happy enough.

NickTomalin's story appeared in the Sunday Times issue of 27th November 1966 and there was uproar. But Mr Fontenoy's wine was a useful step on the learning curve of wine law to the British. I would like to say it could not happen again, but could it?

# 23

# THE WINE THAT DARED NOT SPEAK ITS NAME

This was Algerian wine. The British wouldn't buy it pre-1939 and only a meagre 30 casks a year were imported, and some of these were blended and sold under other names. Algerian wines as such were rarely listed by wine merchants. The French had taken Algeria as a colony in 1842, and there were over a million white settlers, known as "pieds noir" (possibly because they wore black shoes). They had planted tens of thousands of wine acreage to supply the vast vin ordinaire trade in France and other countries. When France capitulated to the Germans in 1940, there was a veritable wine fleet at sea, carrying over ten thousand casks of Algerian red, each containing 660 litres, and these ships sailed into British ports. The volume was so great it filled just about every bonded warehouse in the country; with a Government at loss how to handle it. They consulted various wine importers, of which one, Hallgarten, described this Algerian wine as sound and drinkable. Hallgarten put up several proposals of which one was to sell it as Red Wine, product of France. This was true as Algeria had been made a part of Metropolitan France. In the absence of other wines, the trade gave in and sold the wine, calling it by its correct name. It sold very well and was enjoyed, especially by the London restaurants and clubs. It also improved with age.

During the invasion of Algeria, along with Tunisia in November 1943, the invasion fleet returned to England using casks of Algerian red as ballast. This was sold to pre-war importers of French wines, to their delight, and for the second time the restaurants, clubs and public learned to love Algerian wine. But this rebirth was short-lived. As soon as the British and Americans had liberated France, traders moved fast to import wine from Bordeaux, Burgundy and other areas, and sales of Algerian rapidly diminished. Much of what was left was sold to German wine merchants, who were puzzled that the English would not drink a perfectly good wine but the British customers were not *allowed* to drink it. The importers, to protect their pre-war trade with France, wanted the name "Algerian" to disappear quickly. So that, which was not sold abroad was sold under any name other than Algerian. Also in Germany, when they were able to import from France, any remaining Algerian was sold under other names. The French exporters were as eager to kill the name "Algerian" in Germany as in the UK and they were successful. However, the matter was finally settled by other means.

The refusal of the French European settlers in Algeria, led in 1954 to a bloody war of appalling cruelties on both sides that only ended in 1962 when de Gaulle, in his wisdom, and against the wishes of most of the French people, sensibly gave Algeria its independence. On religious grounds the Algerian Government ordered the destruction of most of the vast area of vineyards planted by the French more than 100 years earlier and in doing so, destroyed also a great source of foreign currency, which they badly needed. An interesting side issue of the Algerian war was that 800,000 of the ex-settlers left for France within six months; an extraordinary mass movement in such a short time.

This was a wine scandal of a particular sort. An unholy alliance of wine merchants, wine shippers and wine growers who deliberately set-out to denigrate, and then destroy the name of a perfectly decent wine they considered harmed their business.

## 24

# HOW ARE THE MIGHTY FALLEN

Mustard, vinegar, Cassis; strange bedfellows for what many people consider to be the grandest of wines. Dijon on the northern edge of the Côte d'Or makes mustard; and jolly good mustard too. Dijon also makes Cassis, a syrup from blackcurrants containing some 10–15% of alcohol, and when mixed with a cool white wine, makes a pleasant aperitif, widely drank in Burgundy, where it is called Kir, named after Canon Kir one time Mayor of Dijon. It is also known by that name in the UK.

Vinegar is the fate often met by even the most famous of wines, which from time to time suffers a bad harvest. Vinegar and Cassis come together in Dijon as components in the making of its splendid mustard. So bad wine and blackcurrants could be said to be the raison d'être for the fame of the little town that makes mustard for a living. A modern Lazarus sitting underneath the table of Dives the wealthy vineyard owner, catching the scraps.

Now, one reason for wine turning into vinegar is bad hygiene in the wine making, but more of that later. Cassis has another use in the red wine game; it is used to add colour, body and some say finesse to cheap wines and, whisper behind your hand, its presence has been seen in the snootiest vineyards on the Côte d'Or from time to time.

In the town of Beaune is the Hospices de Beaune, an ancient and beautiful building usually called the Hôtel Dieu, founded in 1443 by Nicholas Rollin. It has been bequeathed over the years, pieces of many of the best vineyards in Beaune and on the Côte de Nuits. And wine made in these vineyards from the endowment, provides the money needed to maintain the Hospice to succour the poor. Each year on the 3rd weekend in November in a great ceremony, the wines, still in cask are tasted and put up for auction; and the prices obtained tend to establish the prices of the great Burgundies of that year.

On the 23rd November 1976 the auction was held as usual and fetched an average price of £1200 per tonneau of 900 litres; a good price for wine *en primeur*. Naturally the buyers carried out another tasting on receiving their wine in the Spring of 1977, and no fewer than 107 of the 559 tonneau auctioned were found to contain wine well on the way to becoming vinegar. Shock-horror; you could hardly make it up. It was found that because inflation, they said, had put up the price of new casks to £60 each, some vignerons had used old casks for the new wine. Nothing new, or strange, or even wrong about that if, and what an "if", they had been thoroughly cleaned, fumigated and sterilised. The basis of good wine making is good hygiene impeccable cleanliness, and that had not been done; and why? To save a few pence on proper cleaning of old barrels. Should you be strolling through a winery at harvest time, your eye should see evidence of much water, and hoses ready to clean everything and everywhere in readiness for the arrival of the grapes. Its absence should have you thinking about the competence of the winemaker.

The Hospice had no option but to return deposits to the buyers and accept the considerable loss of money for their charitable work. The spoiled wine was sent to Dijon for mustard making, and the Burgundian Wine Authority put out a statement which said that throughout Burgundy almost 20% of the 1976 red wine harvest had suffered some form of "unusual alteration after vinification." Well, they had to say something, didn't they?

In the olden days the Burgundian vignerons' wits were scrambled between terror and greed as he dealt with bad weather. But that was before 1950 *not* in the booming 70's. This was not a case of deliberate fraud; it was no fraud at all, just a sleazy scandal by incompetent greedy winemakers; penny-wise and pound-foolish.

# 25

# BEAUJOLAIS NOUVEAU

**The Perpetual Virgin**

Only in the last 200 years has the Beaujolais been dominated by agriculture. Before the Revolution it was one of the least populated and most miserable regions of France. The division of the large estates after the Revolution, and some road improvements opened new markets in the North. The completion of the Canal de Briare started in 1642 but took generations to complete gave them a cheaper route to Paris, where probably Bcaujolais wine had never been heard of. One has to admit that the region turned-out to be commercial success, mostly because all 6,000 estates and nearly 200 shippers are selling a single wine. There are differences between wines from the South where most of the Beaujolais Nouveau is made and the North where wines such as Morgan and Moulin à Vent are grown. But both of them have one simple, good Beaujolais, which is light and purpley, fruity on the nose and very quaffable. An easy drink and available soon after the harvest is the Nouveàu. The main crop is with the shippers in March and April, and is less quirky, more stable. If you were fortunate enough to be driving, or slithering on the cobbled road which was the Route National Six on a June/July day for preference before the Second World War on the way to Cannes or perhaps Cap Ferrat you would pass the whole of the Beaujolais vineyards on your right extending for about 30 miles from Bellville to a point about 15 miles North of Lyon.

The existence of wine in the region has a long history, but it was a subsistence crop. Each small commune grew for its own use, but post Revolution, the area given over to wine extended to 50,000 acres with 4,000 growers. Though to the neighbours in the posh North, the slopes of the Côte d'Or the Gamay grape was suspect, and its product disliked. It was considered too abundant, too heavy a cropper to make a wine of quality. The absence of roads worthy of the name made the River Saóne essential, easily navigable, as it was to Lyon, which became Beaujolais' principal customer, as it still is. Its arrival in the early 19th century was announced with a notice in every estaminet and restaurant "Le Beaujolais est Arrivé." Strangely, the same notice almost, could be seen in the windows of every London pub and wine bar from 1974 every year. "Le Beaujolais Nouveau est Arrive." And *how* it arrived, continuing to do so until the bubble burst in 2001. In some pubs, the notice would linger from one November to the next, and if any Nouveau was still around it was as dead as a corpse only to be resurrected by the arrival of the next crop. The wine that would not die. Within 6 weeks of harvesting, one of the most superb examples of advertising and public relations, put this quite ordinary red wine into every pub, wine bar and restaurant in London. A glass of it in the hand of every wannabe and poseur who became a connoisseur in one easy lesson. Not only in London but in every capital or large city in Europe – including Paris, who should have known better. For several years on a lovely summer's day. I remember drinking Beaujolais served by the jug in a decent Lyon restaurant, and very cheap it was. But when it reached London as Beaujolais Nouveau, the price had taken an exponential leap, to that of one of the better Bordeaux bourgeois growths. There was a saying said to be popular in France, though I never heard it said "Á Lyon ilya trois fleures Le Rhône Le Saône et Le Beaujolais." But I did hear a Frenchman say cynically "They drink more Beaujolais in Paris than is grown in the Beaujolais."

I once read, by a man whose family had been growing wine for generations and really knew his stuff. "In a very good year such as 1978 the wine (Beaujolais Nouveau) can be a delight to drink, but in most other years, the quality is such as to question the skills of the growers in producing such an unpalatable beverage" but the temptations to produce it by the method called "Maceration Carbonique" are enormous and irresistible; and to have your wine ready for sale in November instead of the next March or April; to have the money flowing in before Christmas; it was almost as good as winning the lottery.

I won't describe the method, but it is simple to practice, though care and thoroughness are required, and the result is quite extraordinary. A drinkable wine becomes ready in a few days, and tastes as though it is a few months old; but beware, its life though not as brief as a mayfly's is disappointingly short.

What irritated me was the uncritical way this arriviste was received by the chattering classes of NW3 and the bevy (or coven) of professional wine writers. A puzzling example of the "king has no clothes" sydrome. Everybody it seemed at the time gagging to be deceived. So, imitating "Disgusted Tunbridge Wells" I wrote a letter in January 1974 to the recently published Decanter magazine and another in February 1990; both about Beaujolais Nouveau, and here they are:-

January 10th, 1974

Sir,
IT WAS A HAPPY day when my wife found the first

issue of Decanter and forthwith bought me a year's subscription. If the style of the letters published is indicative of anything, it is that I am only one of many similarly motivated readers. With that in mind, are there others who like me, groan in disgust when every November the great Beaujolais Fraud rears it's unlovely head again. I refuse to believe that the average wine bibber on tasting vin nouveau, vin d'anèe, or vin bourru as it is sometimes called in Paris, would consider it at best other than an undeveloped wine with the acids and tannin wildly out of balance, at worst damn near vinegar. Yet so much of it appears on the market that it begs the question, does any wine remain in the vats for bottling after a decent interval of time? It goes a long way perhaps to explain why, according to a long accepted legend that in Paris alone, more Beaujolais is drunk than is grown in a single year.

It must rank among the greater triumphs of advertising that a red wine of no great merit, made from the often despised Gamay grape should carry the most widely known name in Anglo-Saxon countries. And moreover, sometimes bearing a price in excess of a decent bourgeois growth claret.

There are perhaps 50,000 acres in the Beaujolais planted with wine, both red and white, which, in an average year yields 125 million bottles. Relate this to the world market and the amount sold, and it might suggest to the meanest of mathematical minds that perhaps the crop is stretched just a teeny weeny bit. But why fuss if a pleasant wine of no great distinction save that from a handful of single vineyards such as Moulin à Vent, Julienas, Fleury and Chiroubles is subjected to creative selling. Better Beaujolais than a fine claret.

Arthur Woods<br>Lindfield, Sussex<br>1990

Sir,

Perhaps 1989 will not only be remembered as the year in which various Communist regimes in Eastern Europe got their come-uppance, but also as the year when the merchants who yearly had flooded the UK with Beaujolais Nouveau accepted that this sad little wine really is mediocre, over-hyped, oversold, and, at a trade price exceeding £1.50 a bottle, an insult to all but the meanest intelligence. It has taken a price rise to over £4 a bottle before these truths, so self-evidence, have at least been accepted, even if for the wrong reasons. In January 1976 I was fortunate to win the *Decanter* monthly letter competition, the prize for which was a tregnum (three-bottles) of Long John Scotch.

The letter's subject was Beaujolais Nouveau, horrors of, price of, absurdity of, and so on. A letter which, in my ignorance, I thought would have provoked howls of rage from the purveyors of this noxious fluid, raised not a whisper – a clever lot, wine shippers, who know when to keep their heads down. Since then, few people sought to criticise this wine, least of all those people who were in the best position to do so. Indeed, every November, as once again the Beaujolais Nouveau signs appeared in swish restaurants and the meanest of pubs, many a brave spirit was ready with a racy 500 words on the splendour of yet another fine harvest.

I never drank that tregnum. Each time I go down into my cellar it catches my eye. Somehow it seemed a pity to broach such a splendid example of the bottle-maker's art. Maybe I'll add a codicil to my Will, suggesting that the bottle be drunk at my wake.

Arthur Woods
Copper Beech Vineyard
Lindfield
West Sussex

Beaujolais reached its peak of popularity in the 1980's with its Beaujolais Nouveau. Urged on by creative marketing, demand outpaced supply. As more Beaujolais growers tried to take advantage of the "Nouveau Craze", production of the traditional Beaujolais dropped and a backlash started in the late 90's and early 21st century. Following the vintage of 2001 more than 1.1 million cases, most of it Nouveau was either destroyed or distilled owing to a huge drop in sales due to customer resistance to Beaujolais Nouveau. This was followed by an article in Lyon Mag, a local newspaper. The French wine critic, François Mauss, claimed in an interview that the reason for the backlash was the poor quality of the Beaujolais Nouveau that had flooded the market for a long time. He claimed that the wine makers had long ignored the warning signs that a backlash was coming, but carried on making what Mauss called *vin de merde* (shit wine). There was shrieks of rage from the Beaujolais producers, and a gathering of 56 co-operative producers filed a lawsuit against the Lyon Mag for publishing Mauss' comments. Rather than sue for libel, the producers sued under an obscure French law that punishes the denigration of French products. In January 2003 the Court at Villefranche sur Saône found in the producers favour and awarded damages of 300,000 Euros, which would have put the small employee owned newspaper out of business. The bad publicity resulting from the "shit wine case" was superb and massive with several international papers, Le Monde, The Times, The New York Times and the Herald Tribune running critical or satirical articles on the Court's decision. Taking the piss out of the shit. In 2005 the highest Court of Appeal found no case for defamation, and the representatives of the wine makers were ordered to pay 2000 Euros in Court costs to Lyon Mag. Justice for once was on the side of the small battalions.

Then there was the Beaujolais Run; a very English institution that started in 1972 and for all I know is still run every year.

It began in 1972 when Sunday Times journalist Alan Hall challenged Fleet Street to "Bring Back the Beaujolais." The object was to find out who could bring it fastest. The RAF settled that lark when they unfairly used a Harrier jet. In 2006 Lord March allowed the Run to make its spiritual home at Goodwood. The event became a five- day show of UK and France affairs. The Beaujolais Run had evolved to become a navigational shoot-out over a checkpoint course in Burgundy. This format ensured Austins & Aston Martins; Jaguar and Jalpa; Porsche & Prius to compete on a level playing field. It provided splendid fun, and plenty of opportunities for sharp practice. Long may it continue, and who the hell cares what is in the bottle anyway!

In 1936 Clochemerle written by Gabriel Chevalier was published in London. The film of the book, long time popular in France was an equal success here, and the tv series in, I think, 1990 equally successful. Clochemerle is a fictional village in the Beaujolais, and over the years hordes of tourists have gone there in an effort to find it. They inevitably fail but many easily identify the real Beaujolais with the fictional. Clochemerle is a classic, and like a good classic reads as fresh today as the day on which it was published. It's Gallic wit and Rabelaisian coarseness loses nothing in the translation. Along with Joseph Heller's Catch 22, but not James Joyce's Ulysses, it is a book I re-read from time to time with unending pleasure. It may not have had the quick dramatic effect on planting Beaujolais on the British psyche as has the emergence of Beaujolais Nouveau; but it will still be read when the Nouveau is but a memory. The book remains on Penguins list of available publications.

# 26

# AUSTRIA & ITS COSY RELATIONSHIP WITH DIETHYLENE GLYCOL

*(don't put it in your car radiator)*

Austria or Germany are easy places to search if you want to find a wine fraud, but there have been so many over the years, they are so easy to find, and it is like shooting ducks in a barrel; they are never outrageous or on a grand scale. At least not until July 1985; the trouble is sweet wines, there are so many, and sweet wines invite trouble and encourage fraud. Moreover the fraud is simple and almost undetectable, unless you are exceptionally greedy, and one such greedy person single-handedly launched the great Austrian anti-freeze wine fraud in 1985. Panic reigned such as had not been seen since the Ottoman Turks were repulsed at the gates of Vienna by the Polish Army led by General Sobieski in 1683.

The role played by sugar in the wine doping game is twofold. You can either add it legally within the chaptalisation system to provide more alcohol during fermentation; and then making it illegal by adding more if the legal percentage allowed does not bring the alcohol up to the necessary minimum level. Or you can add it in a number of ways to make a sweet wine sweeter to push it into a higher price bracket. This might also require the addition of a creative wine label. But the Austrian caper was different, it put the health of the drinker in question, and that was a criminal act.

Non-German speakers are often bewildered by the complicated information on the label of a bottle of German or Austrian wine, and with good reason when faced with the following wine categories of sweet wines.

| | |
|---|---|
| Spätelese | Late picked |
| Auslese | Late picked specially selected |
| Beerenauslese | Late picked of very ripe grapes one by one |
| Trockenbeerenauslese | Grapes picked only when almost dry, exceptionally sweet |

All wines in these categories tend to be expensive, with the last, much more expensive than the first. So by the careful addition of a sweetener, a Spätelese can be promoted to an Auslese and so on. Thus the temptation to engage in fraud is strong and frequently given in to. These practices while well known to those in the trade hardly roused a flutter of concern. The attitude was *caveat emptor*.

In the middle of the 1970's a German biochemist working as a kellermeister discovered that the addition of minute amounts of diethylene glycol increased both body and sweetness into a finished wine; and a cheap wine benefited greatly from the addition. Diethylene glycol is a component in the preparation of anti-freeze used in the radiators of motor vehicles. He was so delighted with his discovery that, deciding there was money in it, he sold the idea to a number of winemakers. Giving him the benefit of the doubt, he did not think that using diethylene glycol held any health risks, and anyway the amount used per litre was so small as to be virtually undetectable. It was *never* observed by investigation until

1985 eleven years later when greed intervened. One of the people involved in the fraud, a wine merchant who sold wine in bulk to Germany, who bought and largely consumed 75% of Austrian production, tried to add to the huge profit he was already making by reclaiming the VAT on the large quantity of diethylene glycol he was purchasing. The local tax inspector was puzzled by the claim on a product of which he had never heard, and smelling a very large rat, contacted the Ministry in Vienna concerned with such matters in December 1984. To extend the metaphor, the cat was now out of the bag and in pursuit of the rat. Five million litres of suspected contaminated wine were seized, the oldest from 1976 vintage and the youngest form 1984, and they were mostly Spätelese, Ausleses and Beerenausleses all from the Burgenland district which is some 20 miles south east of Vienna bordering the Neusiedlersee on the Hungarian frontier. In that area the climate encourages botrytis cinerea, which the French call *la pourriture noble,* the noble rot, and which makes very sweet wines as in Sauternes, the most valuable of all crops. So it was not the handlers of cheap wines that carried out the fraud, but the purveyors of the most expensive. Greed begets greed.

70% of Austrian wine is exported to Germany whether in container, cask or bottle. All unsold wine was put under lock and key; forbidden to be sold. Black Lists were circulated naming exporters and importers; the innocent were punished along with the guilty, for that is always the way of it. White Lists also were published and they also contained names of the guilty along with the innocent. One German importer said he had a million bottles, which though White Listed were un-saleable; and it was reported that the sale of 10,000 million litres was blocked. Always doubt very large numbers, they are usually wrong, but popular with the public. No German merchant would display Austrian wines, and the demand for refunds totalled millions of pounds. Insolvencies multiplied, bankruptcies boomed, long standing businesses ruined, and the reputation of Austrian and German wine in tatters for more than 10 years. German wines from the Rheingau did not escape the smear of scandal though there was no evidence that Rheingau wines had been doctored.

The Austrian Wine Propaganda Office issued a report published in Die Zeit newspaper in July 1985 which included the following "Criminal investigation has been initiated against 52,790 growers, 1582 wine merchants and 52 wine co-operatives." Was anyone left out? In October of the same year, the first Austrian prosecution took place. Otto Hatzy pleaded guilty to adding glycol to 50,000 litres of white wine. Because he confessed he only received a suspended sentence. Hubert Haimerl, an Austrian wine merchant, was jailed for 30 months for doctoring 200,000 litres. Many others were awarded light prison sentences or suspended sentences. Also in 1985 at the Wiesbaden Court, a Mittelheimer grower was charged with illegally blending a 1976 Mittelheimer Beerenauslese with an Austrian wine "to refresh" it. A fine of DM 3600 was imposed, but if the grower agreed to pay, a trial would be avoided. In 1985 that fine expressed in sterling was only about £750. Ranks clearly were closing to save reputations and limit damage to a very important industry.

The UK has in Norwich, a laboratory, owned by the Ministry of Agriculture with a high reputation for accurate analysis and used the new method of Gas Chromatography for investigation. This was a technique for separating and analysing a mixture by passing it through a medium in which the components move at different rates. It was able to determine accurately the presence of diethylene glycol, and the report published said there was no evidence of toxicosity in the level of glycol observed.

In England many of the expensive sweeter wines were withdrawn from sale, and to the great surprise of the Wine Trade some "great names" were included in the list of suppliers.

The whole business stank of panic over a bit of wine doctoring that neither killed nor maimed anyone. It was an international panic, which in its intensity was worse because people should have known better. Villains were sought, but few brought to justice. Yet the adulteration had a life of more than 10 years before the greed of one man caused the exposure. In Austria where gossip, rumour and secret denunciation, are the lifeblood of the people, and where there are those who still believe in the devil and that the Jews killed Christ, it is unlikely that the big names and operators were unknown within the trade. Somebody shouted "panic" so everybody panicked. Could it happen again? Yes it could, because it always does.

But there was one wine that remained unaffected and un-doctored. Why? Because it was too cheap. It is Heurigwein, Heurig means early and is the white wine just out of fermentation, and sold in the weinstuben of Vienna from late October, but particularly in the village of Grinzing, a tramride from the centre, where there are many Heurigehause, of which the most famous is the Schuberthaus in which Schubert drank regularly but could hardly raise the price of a glass. Now Heurigewein at first tastes terrible. It is served in viertals, a viertal is a quarter-litre glass. The second viertal is hardly better; but the 3rd, the 4th and perhaps the 5th are the nectar of the Gods; though not for the faint-hearted. It is then time to take the tram back to

Vienna, a form of transport, which I recommend in the circumstances. Next morning, you will not have a hangover. I promise!

27

# THE GREAT BORDEAUX FRAUD

*(can you tell your Bordeaux from your Beaujolais?)*

The blackest day in the long history of French wine, especially these of the Medoc is surely the 18th December 1974, when the presiding judge in the Bordeaux Court announced a guilty verdict against 8 out of 18 defendants accused of adulterating and falsely labelling at least 3,000,000 litres of wine. A black flag should be permanently flown above the Courthouse. Firstly in shame that members of one of the most famous wine shipping families in Bordeaux was thought to be too grand to be prosecuted for fraud on a massive scale; and secondly that only one man and he, not of the family went to prison. The aristocracy of the cork was humbled by scandal from which it never completely recovered. More than two hundred journalists witnessed their humiliation. The Cruse Family had been in Bordeaux since 1819. Hermann, who came first, was the son of a Lutheran pastor in Schleswig-Holstein when that province was Danish, and the company, Cruse et Fils Frére prospered as merchants and vineyard owners until the present day. The family through intermarriage with other Protestant families became part of a large dynasty of great power within the Bordeaux wine business. And it was two members of the family, Lionel and Yvan, who were put on trial; though the originator and organiser of the fraud was Pierre Bert, who became the most famous and interesting of the 18 defendants. He learned the wine trade, especially the tricky end of it from his grandfather, Louis Bert. The Bert's had many generations of wine-growing behind them but were not of the close-knit few who ran the wine industry and much else in Bordeaux. Pierre's father did a short prison sentence for "economic collaboration" with the enemy. Though he was not unpopular among the wine fraternity, for many of them were equally guilty of continuing to sell to their pre-war German customers. Pierre Bert was extremely popular, considered to be a wit, engaging company, a good friend, and a well-known cutter of corners. To everybody's surprise he pleaded guilty; giving him freedom in court without shame or contrition, to astound everyone there especially the journalists. He blew the gaff on how the growers, brokers and merchants went about their business. He was outrageous, and the public and journalists loved him.

The first step in the "Great Drama", for it deserved that name, was the arrival at the Cruse warehouse on the Quai des Chartrons on 28th June 1973 of a team of inspectors from the Ministry of Finances; a hard-nosed bunch of tax men, smelling blood. The Cruse's were furious. A long established etiquette, by which an inspection was well signalled, had been broken; with no time to bury the bodies before the arrival. 18 months later the trial began on 28th October 1974.

One might almost say that the defendants were forced into fraud. The tremendous hike in Bordeaux prices in 1970/72, which wealthy customers worldwide had been eager to pay; but the merchants had not got the wine quantity to match the orders. There was an analogy with Burgundy, where for generations the small acreage of expensive wines for many years had annually undergone a mythical expansion by doctoring with other lesser wines to meet demand. But Burgundy was a different kettle of fish; peasant growers; not like the haughty Bordeaux bourgeoisie, *sans peur et sans reproche*. The demand in Bordeaux was met by buying via Pierre Bert who supplied lesser wines of decent quality to blend with the expensive Medoc reds, and the blended wines sold to the eager customers at top prices. The inspectors were not so much interested in wine but tax evasion, and they were acting as the police say "on information received." The next visit, again without warning, was to Pierre, and he said, "why hadn't the inspector rung up as in the past? The matter could then have been settled with a handshake and a few thousand francs. After all everyone has been doing this for years, and the inspectors are aware of the facts of life."

There was another crisis about to make the growers' plight even worse. The 1974 harvest had been huge, and there was already a menacing stock of red Bordeaux AOC wines equivalent to one million bottles. So the growers were holding stocks they could not sell to merchants who also had stocks they could not sell to the shippers. All of them had had to pay very high prices to the growers for the harvests of 1970/72. No wonder they were prepared to listen to young Pierre's proposition. He said, either out of the side of his mouth, or some other delicate mode of communication "I can deliver to you as much as you want of quite decent reds, from this place or that, from for example the Midi, complete with the correct acquit vert saying it is bona-fide AOC wine. Now the key to the fraud, without which it would not have been possible was the acquit vert, known as the green docket; which when a grower sells a quantity of AOC wine to a purchaser must accompany the wine to its destination. It is in fact the wine's birth certificate. AOC means Appalation de'Origine Controlée. All decent wines are AOC, so if a grower or a merchant buys a decent, but cheap AOC wine he can with confidence use it to add to a very expensive wine. Or add it to an expensive wine in a cask to replace the wine lost by evaporation, "known as ullage". Even to add a tiny amount declassifies the wine. Now the wine bought by Pierre in the Midi was quite decent but it was not AOC. But Pierre knew how to obtain green dockets, in any number; Bingo!

So Pierre hired a warehouse outside of Bordeaux where he could receive the non-AOC wines he was going to sell on, and he already had the source of green dockets. Wine and docket became married and together were sold to the merchant or grower. That, in essence, was the fraud which Pierre Bert carried out so expertly, and it was so elegant; so exquisite, he deserved to have got away with it. Moreover, although it was only 4 months before the law appeared, the profits reached an annual rate of over a million pounds and sales of 4,000,000 bottles, and his diligence brought him many customers. At that point there were no great names on his list, and cheekily he went to Cruse et Fils Frére. Arriving as a supplicant, somebody below the salt, within a week he became a supplier of status. Pierre's greatest coup, he had captured a great name; the Cruse family no less. He was so trusted that tankers full of Midi wine went direct from the grower, *not* to Pierre's warehouse, but to Cruse complete with the valuable acquit vert. As Claude Cockburn, that great journalist of first the Times and then the Daily Worker said, "No truly honest person was ever deceived."

The trial became a mixture of farce and hilarity; but never tragedy. Pierre was the star, the judge, a crude provincial who knew little about wine, knew little of wine in Bordeaux? What was expected to last 3 days took 3 weeks. Pierre was a natural comic, a deus ex machina, dropped onto the stage as the instrument of justice to punish the great and the good of the Bordeaux wine industry. To expose the hypocrisy of French wine laws and of the merchants who lived so grandly by abusing them. "I am guilty" he said "but I didn't invent the frauds. Thousands of others are just as guilty, and for generations." Accused of mixing wines, he said "It's common practice; it's called 'baptism'. The better Clarets often contain a bit of Algerian." That was like accusing the Pope of being a Protestant!

A devastating headline in a national paper read "Experts can't tell Claret from Plonk". The court was thronged with lawyers; even the Midi growers were represented, and their lawyers said that half the Midi production is sold regularly to the shippers in Bordeaux and Burgundy to emerge in bottles bearing valuable labels. On reading *that* the British and American tasters and writers must have been choking on their Margaux and Latour. More reputations were destroyed at that trial than you could throw a stick at; and more damning, some say dangerous, information about an ancient trade saw the light of day than was good for it. But it had to be said. It was a very serious trial. Fraud endangers us all, but the result was pure pathos; and the punishments pathetic. The French Establishment closed ranks, the politicians came to the rescue to save a few necks and the honour of France. But the Bordelaise enjoyed the discomfiture of the Cruse family and the members of their extended family. Only 8 out of 18 defendants received sentences and only Pierre went to prison – for one year.

Lionel and Yvan Cruse received 1 year suspended sentence, 3 years on probation and a trifling fine of 27,000 Francs.

The other 5 were only walk-on players and received

small, suspended sentences. But there was clemency after appeals. The suspended sentences of the Cruse's were quashed. Pierre's sentence was reduced to 6 months and he was allowed to carry on his work in the daytime, only to return to the prison at night. Pierre Bert reminds one of that other faker, Hans van Meegeren, the Dutch artist who was such a good forger of Vermeers and others, his principal customers were Hermann Goering, and other Nazi scoundrels.

Both Bert and van Meegeren became folk heroes, which pleased me. However, when a villain like Pierre is treated so leniently, there is clearly no danger in the wine adulteration and false labelling racket. I am told that the sales of the great Medoc reds, and the prices, are now higher than ever.

# 28

# THE RODENSTOCK JEFFERSON AFFAIR

*(or the great Lafite 1787 scam)*

Believe only half of what you hear, and have strong doubts about the other half. That should have been the guiding principle of those in contact with Hardy Rodenstock in this farcical, childlike fraud. There was a man called Meinhard Goerke; said to have been an apprentice labourer with German Railways by somebody who wrote a book about this fraud. I do wish writers' had a better knowledge of English. An apprentice is a young man, or used to be, chosen for training as a skilled man in an honourable trade. A labourer is a hod-carrier; a tea-maker and a dogsbody for the skilled man. He gave this up and worked on showbiz periphery as a pop band gofer. He then metamorphed into wine connoisseur of old and rare wines without any training. Thinking a change of name would give confidence to future clients, he chose to call himself Hardy Rodenstock, which just happened to be the name of a wealthy family involved in the optics industry. Perhaps he is related, but that is one of the many unknowns about this man. Of one thing not in doubt is, he had plenty of friends, not short of influence, for by 1980 he was the host to many wine tasting parties with impressive guest lists, at which many wines of distinction were tasted. The apotheosis, one might even venture "deification" came in 1985 when he claimed to have made an astounding find in the Marais district of central Paris. The Marais is quite near to Notre Dame. Whether he claimed to have made the find, or was just given information about it, also, is not clear. Workers, it is said, broke through a wall in the basement of an old house to find a cache of wine which turned out to be from some of the greatest vineyards in the Medoc communes of Bordeaux and the bottles were marked with the names of Lafite, Margaux, Brane-Mouton and Château d'Yquem (which is in the Sauternes). No labels of course, but the names were marked on the bottle with the engraved initials Th:J- which Rodenstock said were the initials of Thomas Jefferson, 3rd President of America, and Minister Plenipotentiary in France from 1785 to 1794. He really had pulled a rabbit out of the hat. The bottles were marked with vintage years of 1784 and 1787, and one of them a Lafite 1787 was auctioned at Christies in London, and it was knocked-down quickly to Christopher Forbes of the Forbes Corporation in New York, for £105,000, five times the previous price for a bottle of wine at auction. The date was 2nd December 1985, and this bottle was sold by the most renowned auction house in the world, Christies, to a rich American company who presumably had not become rich by stupidity, on the say-so of a virtually unknown German, that the bottle was originally the property of Thomas Jefferson, the 3rd President of America. Rodenstock would not say where the wine cache was found, when it was found, or from whom it was purchased. If there is evidence that before, during or after the auction he was severely questioned to provide what would normally be considered necessary information about the cache, it has not been published.

In June 1986 Michael Broadbent, taster in chief at Christies, attended Château Mouton Rothschild where

Rodenstock was to preside at the opening of a 1787 bottle of Brane-Mouton. Broadbent reported the event in the September 1986 issue of Decanter, and his description, his prose was awesome; worthy of a more famous occasion such as the breaking through to the tomb of Tut'ankhamun at Thebes by Howard Carter. The cork was removed, the bottle cracked a little and the contents tasted. Nineteen were present, mostly German friends, and Jancis Robinson, a wine writer, young and to whom I gave then, and now, rather more respect than I would accord to the old brigade. Everybody considered it remarkable that this Claret of 1787 should so have survived nearly 200 years and still be drinkable; but of course it was not that old as the future was to reveal. It crossed my mind when reading Broadbent's article that Rodenstock's gift for showmanship might have led him to arrive at the tasting, clad in the medieval armour of a Teutonic Knight on a white stallion. The tasting was a success, a great success, and Michael Broadbent said "There's not a trace of decay. It's not acidic, nor oxidised, and it's quite genuine, there's no doubt about that." Rodenstock must have been relieved a gathering of the great and the good had given him their seal of approval. And he *still* refused to say how and when the wine came into his possession. It was now six months since the Christies auction. Plenty of time to have investigated ruthlessly the background of Rodenstock. For there were other bottles still to be sold.

It so happened that while the wine-world was praising and talking about Rodenstock, I was in correspondence with an old friend in South Carolina, Robert de Treville Lawrence III, whose ancestors and those of his wife were acquaintances of Thomas Jefferson. Lawrence was an amateur winegrower, a Jefferson scholar and publisher of a book "Jefferson and Wine", and desperately wanted the

Rodenstock wine find to be genuine. My disbelief pained him but did not harm our friendship. Jefferson's house at Monticello is a museum, complete with curator and staff, who know more about the 3rd President of America than anybody and have a vast library of his papers, diaries, and especially those concerned with wine, in particular French wine. They tried with diligence and enthusiasm to uncover evidence on wine purchases that might have ended-up in Paris, and hidden. They failed to find anything. But this failure had no influence on the "true believers". It never does. When people desperately want to believe, and Rodenstock had many disciples, they behave like flat earthers, and who ever persuaded a single one of them that the earth is round? Though Eric de Rothschild of Château Lafite said "As always in such cases, it is possible that this bottle be a fake, but in which case, it would be a particularly good one." Unluckily or luckily it would be impossible to prove one way or the other its authenticity." Precisely; well, as events proved, not quite, and a time bomb with Rodenstock's name on it was being assembled in the USA. Mr William Koch, heir to an oil fortune and of a litigious nature; he spent years in court fighting his brothers for his inheritance, bought 4 of the alleged Jefferson bottles through Farr Vintners, a London broker, acting for Rodenstock, paying $500,000 in the late '80's. He already had a cellar-load of wine, numbering many thousands of bottles, so it is said, and decided to do what others, equally involved should already have done, set about investigating Rodenstock; employing a team of gumshoes, led by an ex FBI man, and including an ex Scotland Yard detective. He spent over $1,000,000 on the investigation, and filed a lawsuit in New York against Rodenstock. A New York journalist named Howard Goldberg who, like me, had been an unbeliever from the start wrote "If a court finds that

Rodenstock fabricated the famous Th:J- initials, if there was neither a walled cellar in Paris where mysteriously a cache of Jefferson's bottles were discovered; if the Lafite and Brane-Mouton bottles that cost Koch $500,000 were plonk with a Ph.D., what on earth has been in those bottles?"

In 1992 roughly concurrent with the Koch investigation, Rodenstock was in trouble again, much nearer home. He had sold a bottle of the claimed 1787 Lafite to a fellow German collector, Hans-Peter Fredericks, who disputed its provenance and sent it for analysis to the German Institute of Environmental and Health Research. Tests for the radio-isotope carbon 14 and tritium were made, which showed that at least half the wine in the bottle was from the year 1962 or later. Rodenstock, combative as ever, said the bottle must have been tampered with to discredit him.

Michael Broadbent of Christies said "Another bottle is to be analysed, but until the German Courts have sorted out who topped-up the disputed bottle, there's not much to say. I just wish Hardy Rodenstock would say how he came by these bottles. It's doing a tremendous amount of damage to the old, fine, and rare market." Oh dear, oh dear, if only Mr Rodenstock would fade away.

*"As I was going up the stair*
*I met a man who wasn't there*
*He wasn't there again next day*
*Oh how I wish he'd go away"*

But he wouldn't, and he didn't.

In the New York restaurant, it is said, that another Jefferson bottle was destroyed when a waiter accidentally kicked it over. Was it being heated-up against a hot radiator? An old waiter's trick.

The Koch case continued for a very long time, and much of Rodenstock's past was uncovered, including evidence the engraved initials were done with a modern power tool. But Rodenstock maintained that the New York Court had no jurisdiction over him, and the Court agreed, in the Autumn of 2006. Since then, Koch filed another suit and in March 2009 the judge re-opened the case and, as far as I know, it had not finished yet. I'm beginning to admire Rodenstock.

Christies mystify me. Founded in 1766 and highly successful and streetwise up until the present day, and if they were fooled by Rodenstock it must have been because it suited them. Why would that be? And Forbes to whom £105,000 was no more than petty cash probably wanted to be known as the owner of the most expensive bottle of wine in the world. He was, but not for long. Does the ghost of Rodenstock still stalk the wine cellars to terrify the haughty tasters and endanger their reputations? It is said that the 19th century Bourbons forgot nothing yet learned nothing. So why were those duped by Rodenstock not alerted by *the great Bordeaux Fraud of 1973/74*?

But the best and most farcical happening of this wine scandal (it can't be called a fraud because it has not yet been proved a fraud beyond a peradventure), reached its apogee, 6 months after Forbes bought his bottle at the Christies auction of December 1985. In the words of Michael Broadbent himself "Just before the Brane-Mouton tasting I received a telephone call from the Forbes Museum in New York to say that the cork of the 1787 Lafite had dropped into the wine. A pity, but hardly surprising since it was displayed under spotlights which will have heated, dried out and further shrunk the cork."

On reading this, a wry smile might have formed on my face as I remembered that aphorism of Oscar's "Only a man with a heart of stone would not have laughed on hearing of the death of Little Nell."

# 29

# POSTSCRIPT

This book could have been much longer, but I wanted it to be concise, tidy and adequate, covering the core subjects of the background to the Anglo Saxon and Anglo Irish people, which migrated, not from poverty or persecution to certain wine growing countries of Europe. There, in certain areas they took the indigenous growers metaphorically by the scruff of the neck and transformed them from cottage industries into great international affairs with reputations that have withstood the wear and tear of several centuries. Additionally, I wanted to investigate enough of the historical background of wine to explain the drama, confusion and sometimes egregious practices that from time to time sullied the reputations of an extraordinary collection of tough intuitive and sometimes very brave people. Inevitably because such people hold the opinion that the law is for lesser breeds, fraud and scandals are on occasions revealed to the delight of their many enemies within their own trade.

Bearing in mind the hauteur, which seems natural to many Bordeaux vineyard owners, brokers and négociants, the greatest of all the wine scandals that exploded like a thunderbolt on the Bordeaux Law Courts in December 1974 all but brought them to their knees. Particularly as the cutting of the expensive Medoc wines with powerful reds from other regions had been going on for generations. It had been widely practised in the best-known vineyards of Burgundy for even longer.

Paradoxically it was the British market from the 17th century that encouraged the French growers in Bordeaux to strengthen their Clarets, which were considered insipid and too low in alcohol for English palates. What they wanted was something closer to the port, widely drunk in London, Dublin and Edinburgh. So the French, always sensitive to a client's needs, cut their Clarets with powerful reds imported from Spain and the South of France, then added a percentage of grape brandy to be on the safe side. Thus was the tradition of meaty, alcoholic Burgundies, and Clarets suitable for men rather than girls born in England. It is beyond belief that this dishonest doctoring of expensive wines was unknown; but it is also true that the wines of Bordeaux, and later of the Côte de Nuits and Côte de Beaune greatly benefited from the judicious additions of reds from sunnier climes.

However, Hubris always finally, attracts the attention of Nemesis and as Mary the Mother of Christ when she praised God said:

*"He had put down the mighty from their seats and exalted those of low degree"*

Those of "low degree" were numerous, and finally arrived in the form of Australians and New Zealanders with scant regard for tradition who set about kicking the merde out of the French growers with their brilliant reds and whites. Gallic pride and amour-propre had been hurt; not once but twice by, as de Gaulle used to call us "Les Anglo Saxons." First in the 18th and 19th centuries when the Anglos came to Bordeaux to turn their cottage industry into an international business. Second in the last 20 years by their crude British sheep farmers from the Southern Hemisphere, who greatly damaged the French UK sales. I was amused to read in the Daily Telegraph of 9th January 2010 a piece headed "French accused of trying to pass off wine as Kiwi;" and here is the article in full.

### FRENCH ACCUSED OF TRYING TO PASS OFF WINE AS KIWI
By Bonnie Malkin in Sydney
and Henry Samuel in Paris

THE FRENCH have long regarded their vineyards as the toast of the wine world.

But in a humiliating blow to Gallic pride, winemakers have been accused of trying to pass off their bottles as New Zealand produce to cash in on the popularity of antipodean brands.

A tribunal in Australia has ruled that Lacheteau, based in the Loire Valley, labelled its sauvignon blanc Kiwi Cuvee in a nod to the quirkily-named New Zealand and Australian white wines.

The Wine has been sold in British and European supermarkets, but when the company attempted to register the brand in Australia, New Zealand winemakers objected.

The New Zealand Winegrowers Association opposed the registration and a hearing decided the name was likely to deceive and confuse consumers.

France is renowned for fiercely protecting the right of its winemakers to use regional names and geographic indicators on bottles.

The country also defends its regional specialities through its *Appellation d'origine contrôllée,* or AOC system, which protects more than 300 wines, including Bordeaux and Chablis, as well as 161 French foods.

## A fight against the English invasion

The invasion of English words poses a greater "threat" to France's national identity than the imposition of German under the Nazi occupation, a group of French patriots claim. *Avenir de la langue français* (Future of the French language) and eight other groups writing in two national newspapers, *Le Monde* and *l'Humanité*, called on the government yesterday to stop the Anglo onslaught. They said: "There are more English words on the walls of Paris than German words under the [Nazi] Occupation."

They said Nicholas Sarkozy, the president, was obsessed with making France bi-lingual.

The French wine industry has been hit by falling domestic consumption and stiff competition from the New World. Australian wine has overtaken French fare as Britain's favourite tipple.

Part of the success of wines from Australia and New Zealand has been attributed to their catchy names and emblems, which often use animals and birds, known as "critter labelling".

Jeffrey Davies, a Bordeaux wine expert, said that there was a "nasty irony" about a French producer muscling in on New Zealand's success and it was a sign that Kiwis had "beaten the French at their own game".

"This is an extension of the phenomenon of 'critter labels' that the New World has marketed in the US and Europe," he said. "In order to capture market share in the New World, the French have been doing the same

"I don't know whether this reflects a superior quality among New Zealand sauvignon blanc or their ability to better market their wines".

Lacheteau's label stated that it was a French product and it tried to claim "Kiwi" was not a colloquialism.

The New Zealand Winegrowers Association said the bottle clearly emulated antipodean products. "Sauvignon blanc is the archetypal New Zealand wine variety and screw cap bottles such as [Lacheteau] uses, while being the preferred choice for New Zealand wines, are anathema to traditional French winemakers."

There is nothing like competition to improve the quality and availability of a product whether wine or motorcars; and its is as true today as it was in the 18th century when that economist and philosopher Adam Smith wrote of "The invisible hand of the market." France and other European wine growing countries will respond to the challenges of the newer and younger wine makers, as they will need to do to satisfy the great thirst of China and India for the wines of vitisvinifera.

# SELECTED FURTHER READING

*The Great Vintage Book,* Michael Broadbent
*Madeira,* Rupert Croft-Cook
*The Factory House At Oporto,* John Delaforce
*The Wine Masters,* Nicholas Faith
*Burgundy,* Anthony Hanson
*Dionysus A Social History Of Wine,* Edward Hyams
*Vin,* Edward Hyams
*Sherry,* Julian Jeffs
*Jefferson On Wine,* Robert de Treville-Lawrence
*Wines Of France,* Alexis Lichine
*Portugals Wines & Winemakers,* Richard Mayson
*The Wines Of Bordeaux,* Edmund Denning-Rowsell
*Wines & Vineyards Of France,* René Poulain & Louis Jacqelin
*Le Beaujolai,* Hubert Piat
*Le Goût Du Vin,* Emile Peynaud
*Connaissance Et Travail Du Vin,* Emile Peynaud
*The Discovery Of France,* Graham Robb
*Confessions Of A Wine Lover,* Jancis Robinson
*Encyclopedia Of Wine,* Frank Schoonmaker